The Eight Treasures™ Energy Enhancement Exercise

By Maoshing Ni, C.A., D.O.M., Ph.D.
With Preface and Commentaries by Hua-Ching Ni

SEVEN STAR
COMMUNICATIONS
SANTA MONICA

This book is designed to be used together with the *Eight Treasures*™ (VHS) videotape also available from SevenStar Communications.

The College of Tao offers teachings on the Universal Integral Way of health and spirituality based on the teachings of Hua-Ching Ni. To obtain a list of Mentors teaching in your area or country, or if you are interested in teaching, please write to the Universal Society of the Integral Way, PO Box 28993, Atlanta, GA 30358-0993 USA.

Acknowledgments:
   To my father, Hua-Ching Ni, without whom this knowledge would not have been preserved and passed down.
   Thanks and appreciation to John Barber, Rick Baudino, Clinton Choate, Claire and Peter Cunneen, Nadia Dayao, John Decker, Janet DeCourtney, Steve Gettier, Karina Herring, Frank and Micki Iborra, Mark Johnson, Seokjin Kim, Neil Malley, Linda Modaro, Christi Peralta, John Rugis, Paul Sheldon, Tiane Sommer, San Gee Tam and Blair Taylor for contributions to and assistance with preparing this book, and to the many students who gave their valuable feedback.

Published by: SevenStar Communications
1314 Second Street
Santa Monica, California 90401

The calligraphy in this book was done by Hua-Ching Ni. The photographs of Maoshing Ni were taken in 1985. Printed on acid-free paper.

First Printing February 1996

The Eight Treasures™ is a trademark of SevenStar Communications used to denote the series of exercises described in this book. This series of exercises and the name "Eight Treasures" are legally protected under all applicable United States and international laws relating to trademarks, copyright, and intellectual property. The Eight Treasures is the property of SevenStar Communications, and instruction of the exercises or use of the name by anyone not expressly authorized by SevenStar Communications is forbidden. Anyone wishing to teach or otherwise use the name "Eight Treasures" must contact SevenStar Communications to ask permission.

Library of Congress Cataloging-in-Publication Data
Ni, Maoshing.
      The Eight Treasures / by Maoshing Ni : with preface and commentaries by Hua-Ching Ni.
            p.   cm.
      Includes bibliographical references and index.
      ISBN 0-937064-74-2
      1. Ch' i kung. I. Title.
RA781.8.N5   1994
613.7'1--dc20

94-30068
CIP

*Dedicated to all who aspire to optimal well-being
and the way of spiritual immortality.*

To all readers,

According to the teaching of the Universal Integral Way, male and female are equally important in the natural sphere. This fact is confirmed in the diagram of *T'ai Chi*. Thus, discrimination is not practiced in our tradition. All of our work is dedicated to both genders of the human race.

Wherever possible, constructions using masculine pronouns to represent both sexes are avoided. Where they occur, we ask your tolerance and spiritual understanding. We hope that you will take the essence of these teachings and overlook the limitations of language. Gender discrimination is inherent in English. Ancient Chinese pronouns do not differentiate gender. We hope that all of you will achieve yourselves well beyond the level of language and gender. Thank you.

Warning - Disclaimer

This book is intended to present information and techniques that have been in use throughout the Orient for many years. This information and these practices utilize a natural system within the body; however, no claims are made regarding their effectiveness. The information offered is according to the author's best knowledge and experience and is to be used by the reader at his or her own discretion and liability.

Because of the sophisticated nature of the information contained within this book, it is recommended that the reader also study other books by the author and by Hua-Ching Ni for a broader understanding of energy-conducting exercises and a healthy lifestyle.

People's lives have different conditions and their growth has different stages. Because the background of people's development cannot be unified, no single practice is universally applicable for everyone. Thus, it must be through the discernment of the reader that practices are selected. The adoption and application of the material in this book must therefore be the reader's own responsibility.

The author and publisher of this book are not responsible in any manner for any harm that may occur through following the instructions in this book.

Contents

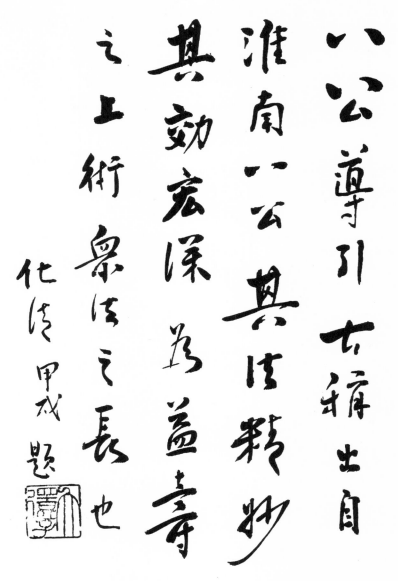

八公尊引古籍出自
淮南八公其法精妙
其効宏深為益壽
之上術衆法之長也

化清 甲戌 題

This energy conducting exercise
　　originated with the Eight Immortals
　　in the region of Huei Nang
　　during the Han Dynasty.
The practice is well-refined.
Its effects are deep and far-reaching.
It is an effective way to lengthen your years.
Among similar types of chi gong practices
　　this is the best for a broad range of people.

List of Figures

The Eight Treasures™

Warm Up

1. Sustaining Heaven with Both Hands to Adjust the Three Warmers
   a. Move the Stars and Turn the Big Dipper
   b. The Great Elephant Raises Its Trunk
   c. The Dolphin's Fins Pat the Water
   d. Bringing the Sea to the Top of the Mountain
   e. Water and Fire Meet

2. Drawing the Bow with Both Hands to Aim at a Distant Target
   a. The Great Bird Spreads Its Wings
   b. Drawing the Bow
   c. The Unicorn Turns Its Head to Look at the Moon
   d. Drawing the Precious Sword from Its Sheath
   e. Moving the Mountain and Pouring Out the Sea

3. Raising the Hands to Adjust the Stomach and Spleen
   a. The Jade Plate Receives the Morning Dew
   b. Looking at the Lotus Flower in the Clear Pond

4. Turning Your Head to Tonify the Nervous System
   a. Turning the Head to Look at Your Star
   b. Turning the Head to Contemplate Earth
   c. The Weeping Willow Shivers in the Early Morning Breeze

5. Swaying the Spinal Column to Take Away Heart Fire
   a. The Sleeping Lion Shifts Its Head and Awakens
   b. Lying Down to Watch the Constellations

6. Raising the Heels to Remove Physical and Mental Weakness
   a. Bringing the Stream Back to the Sea
   b. Pumping the Water from the Origin of the Fountain

7. Tightening the Tendons to Reinforce Yourself
   a. Pushing Down the Fierce Tiger
   b. The Tiger Grabs Its Prey
   c. Clench the Teeth, Widen the Eyes and Strike in the Four Directions
   d. The Tiger Gathers Its Energy and Crouches

8. Grabbing the Ankles to Strengthen Your Vital Force
   a. The White Crane Washes Its Wing Feathers
   b. The White Crane Turns Its Head to Look Up
   c. The White Crane Twists Its Body to Look Up
   d. The White Crane Sharpens Its Beak
   e. The White Crane Strengthens Its Vital Force
   f. The White Crane Stretches Its Legs Behind and Forward
   g. The White Crane Guards the Plum Flower Proudly Standing Alone on the Cold Mountain
   h. The White Crane Limbers Its Wings
   i. The Dragon Flies Throughout the Heavens

Gathering the Chi (Standing Meditation)

Section 1

Introduction
to the Eight Treasures™

The Unicorn Turns Its Head to Look at the Moon
(Figure 1)

Preface

by Hua-Ching Ni

The Eight Treasures™ (仙家八景圖) are called *Shien Jia Ba Duan Jin* in Chinese, meaning "The Eight Groups of Exercise From the Immortal School." I also refer to these movements as the simplified form of *Ba Gong Dao-In*, which means "Energy-Conducting Exercises of the Eight Old Ones." They have also been called the "Practice of the Eight Immortals," and became more widely known after Prince Liu An encouraged people to use them as a way to integrate the body with the mind and spirit.

The simplified form of the Eight Treasures is more popular than the original form of *Ba Gong Dao-In*. Later, the Eight Treasures were combined with *kung fu* to become *t'ai chi ch'uan*. Eight Treasures is a good foundation for learning *t'ai chi* because it is easier for people to learn, clears energy blockages, strengthens *chi*, and teaches the fundamentals of movement.

This practice should not be confused with the common "Eight Pieces of Brocade." The Eight Treasures are from the immortal tradition, passed down through many generations to the Ni family lineage.

All types of *dao-in* or energy-conducting exercises were initiated and continually developed in China. The Eight Treasures were formally organized around 2,000 years ago, but the original movements, which are much older, developed from the *dao-in* exercises practiced by ancient achieved people who lived in accordance with nature and believed in good health as an essential component of spiritual enlightenment. They sought to integrate body with mind and spirit. Through the development and routine practice of specific techniques such as the Eight Treasures, they were able to refine their energies and cultivate themselves spiritually.

About 4,600 years ago, on the Yellow River plateau, the chief of the Lai tribe defeated an invasion by the Ci Yo tribe, and at last united the many tribes of China. This chieftain was the famous Yellow Emperor whom all Chinese regard as the founding father of the vast empire of China.

From the Yellow Emperor, many arts and crafts and vast knowledge were passed down through generations to the 20th century. These became the basis of Chinese culture, especially the arts of health and longevity that are found in the classical texts on

Chinese medicine[1] that were collected and written down around 400 B.C.E.[2] At that time, preventive medicine was the stepping stone to health and longevity, and proper exercise was an integral part of it.

Around 205 C.E., during the time of Master Kou Hong, who was also known as Pao Poh Tzu, there were thousands of special *chi kung (chi gong)* practices that expressed the different kinds of spiritual energy that people have. However, one's spiritual energy should serve one's life, not be exchanged for money or fame. Learning the Eight Treasures can help guide your energy to a higher level of refinement.

The importance of guiding energy is illustrated by the following story. In ancient times, there were great floods that happened during the time of Niao (2357-2258 B.C.E.), Shun (2257-2208 B.C.E.) and Yu (2205-2197 B.C.E.). Yu's father tried to resolve the flooding by attempting to dam the flow of water. That did not work well. Yu's method was to guide the flow of water in the right direction: to the ocean.

Sometimes we use this story as a metaphor for a person who has too much sexual desire. Most people's sexual energy is too strong. Allowing it to become or remain uncontrolled, like flooding, dissipates your energy and leads to general weakness, health problems and premature aging. But just like trying to stop water, if you try to stop your sexual energy by not having sex, which is what general religions tell you to do, this only causes the sexual energy to transform into all kinds of health problems and mental and emotional trouble. Thus it does not work well. In our metaphor, the ocean signifies Tao, the Way. So you need to guide your sexual energy and transform it correctly. Our energy comes from the ocean of Tao, and returns to Tao, the great nature.

We all know that ocean water evaporates to become clouds in the sky, which eventually turn into rain, and the rain causes saturation of lands as in irrigation or flooding. When the water is guided back to the ocean, the process of circulation is complete. The result is a beautiful, harmonized earth with productive land that provides all things for all lives.

---

[1]Editor's Note: See *The Yellow Emperor's Classic of Medicine,* a new translation of the *Neijing Suwen* with commentary by Maoshing Ni.

[2]C.E. stands for Common Era and B.C.E. stands for Before Common Era. The distinction is the same as between A.D. and B.C.

The same type of process takes place within you. Your sexual or reproductive energy is the source of your bodily energy, and it builds internally. If you just meditate every day, however, without practicing physical energy conducting, your mind will become wild or scattered. You might try to control the mind with prayers or mantras, but objectively and realistically, they do not guide your energy correctly.

By learning the Eight Treasures, you learn to control your wild or bodily energy. Then by continuing to practice, you can also build more energy. Control is the first step; building more energy is the second step. Practicing the Eight Treasures also unifies the body and mind so you become calm and focused, and use the form to develop to higher levels. You might be interested in reading my book, *Strength From Movement: Mastering Chi*, which discusses various forms of movement practice and their benefits, including the Eight Treasures.

Standing, moving and sitting techniques are all used for guiding energy, but there are still other internal energy-conducting methods that are described in *The Workbook for Spiritual Development of All People*. There are many different forms of gathering and conducting energy. Because human life has different spheres of energy, it is necessary to guide and manage all of them correctly for effective and positive use. Therefore, in addition to learning and practicing the Eight Treasures, you may wish to read my other books for more information about guiding, developing and refining your personal energy.

Traditional Chinese Medicine was developed by the ancient achieved ones. There is an old saying that a good healer cures the problem before it happens. The mediocre healers can only resolve a problem that has already happened. This can be understood as the standard level of healing work. If you do the Eight Treasures, you can not only eliminate problems but also prevent a problem from happening. This is the best health care you can provide for yourself. You might read my book *The Power of Natural Healing* to attain other necessary knowledge about self-care.

Modern students know the advantages and disadvantages of modern technological and material achievements. If they can also learn the truthful spiritual achievement of ancient people, then they can develop more easily and have better lives without needing to start all over from the beginning again. Even if you view the world and life differently than the ancients, the basic foundation of natural life has not changed. Modern technology may offer more external conveniences, but people still do not understand their own inner life completely. Learning the Eight Treasures is a beginning step.

Although scientists turn away from religion because it is fantasy, they must admit that human nature has a psychological aspect. Religions have contributed to some people's psychological lives, but religion is not truthful or objective enough. If you believe in a religion and still remain objective, then you will not be a good religious follower, because religion does not require or promote objectivity. This is the difference between following a religion and learning the Integral Way.

What the Integral Way, with practices such as the Eight Treasures, offers is the continual spiritual development of your own life and human culture as a whole. It is objective and realistic. I have carefully filtered the enormous heritage of the ancient society, at least in China, where there are 4,000 years of written language development. I hope that all of you can find something realistic in my work that will be helpful to your life. You do not necessarily need to believe what I believe; you can choose your own interpretation.

We practice the Eight Treasures because each life is a small model of nature. You can believe it or not; I do not need you to be my follower or student. You can become my friend, even if you believe differently. As a modern person, you might use more machinery than I do, but machines still have not replaced nature. We offer the Eight Treasures so that you can experience their benefits for your own natural and complete self-development.

Chapter 1

What Are the Eight Treasures?

The Eight Treasures are comprised of eight sets of movements that combine toning and strengthening exercises, stretching, and specific breathing techniques for the purpose of maintaining health and preventing disease. It is an ancient system of energy-enhancement based on the natural motion of the heavenly bodies. This is one way of experiencing that each life is a small model of nature. Moving the body in this fashion guides your internal energies to flow according to the same natural laws that keep the planets on course and the galaxies propelling through space harmoniously.

This series of harmonized movements is governed by the principle of *yin* and *yang*. Do not view them as unrelated or separate, different postures. They are designed to open and circulate your *chi*, your vital energy, systematically throughout your body. The practice is also an excellent foundation for *t'ai chi*.

The Eight Treasures are a type of internal exercise (*chi gong* or *dao-in*). *Chi gong* (*chi kung*) consist of a series of movements, both internal and external, that directly activate or facilitate a smooth flow of *chi* or vital force throughout the body. *Chi gong* specifically combines breathing techniques, simple movements, postural training and mental imagery to guide the flow of energy. In this way, it releases tension and stimulates vitality, thus promoting self-healing within the body and strengthening the immune system against the onset of disease and imbalance.

This kind of exercise is how you can take responsibility for your health and for your whole life, internally and externally.

The 32 individual movements of Eight Treasures resemble various aspects of nature. Names such as "The Dolphin's Fins Pat the Water," "The Great Bird Spreads Its Wings," and "The Weeping Willow Shivers in the Early Morning Breeze" illustrate the natural, creative movements of the exercises.

How Were the Eight Treasures Developed?

The Eight Treasures are one of the ancient methods of self-cultivation in the Tradition of the Union of Tao and Man. Its roots are prehistoric, being one of the treasured arts passed down from the Yellow Emperor.

Who Can Benefit?

The Eight Treasures can be practiced by anyone at any level of fitness. It is non-impact, simple, and appropriate for all ages. People with severe health problems can benefit from practicing the method of breathing, and placing less emphasis on the physical aspect. As one's health improves, the more physical aspect of the exercises can be added. People who are already in excellent physical condition can benefit by developing a strong center (abdominal *chi*) and a more harmonious flow of energy.

Practicing the Eight Treasures is like handwriting: each individual expresses his or her own personality. The gentle, internally-focused movements can be adapted to personal differences. Each individual can also adjust their practice to fit their stage of learning.

What Are the Benefits?

Through a process of development and refinement over generations, the Eight Treasures has become a complete practice that benefits the whole body from head to toe. No part of the body is overlooked. The movements help unblock obstructions in your energy channels, thus promoting a smooth energy flow throughout the entire body. The sensations felt during and after the exercise are like simultaneously having a complete massage and a good workout. It is also an excellent foundation for *t'ai chi* practice, because it unblocks and improves your energy (*chi*) before you use *t'ai chi* for *chi* circulation.

The therapeutic value of gentle energy guidance exercises has been recognized in China for thousands of years, but only recently has it been acknowledged in the West as a means of restoring both physical and mental health. Consistent practice of the Eight Treasures as *chi gong* improves internal energies so effectively that the indirect result in many cases has been the curing of a wide variety of disorders.

With regular practice, students will first feel the benefit in areas about which they are most sensitive or aware. Usually the changes that are first noticed are a calmer mind and more relaxed body. As the practice deepens, you may also develop a stronger immune system with decreased susceptibility to colds and other infections. Continued practice leads to the gradual correction of significant preexisting imbalances within the body.

The Eight Treasures not only promote an increase in energy,

flexibility, and balance; they can also improve the quality of life and feeling of well-being by integrating the body, mind and spirit. Studies have shown that daily practice of the Eight Treasures helps reduce stress and tension, increases immunity, raises your energy level, lowers blood pressure, invigorates the cardiovascular system, improves circulation, balances blood sugar levels and improves metabolism, along with many other benefits. It improves digestion, regulates the nervous system, enhances the respiratory system, and increases the motor functions.

Therefore, besides being a fundamental exercise for *t'ai chi* movement and all martial arts, Eight Treasures are also practiced for healing purposes. It assists the body's own innate healing powers to correct conditions such as neurasthenia, hypertension, low blood pressure, insomnia, asthma, emphysema, coronary heart disease, poor circulation, indigestion, poor appetite, degenerative motor functions, incoordination, arthritis, partial numbness and paralysis of the extremities, and countless others. Psychologically and spiritually, they increase awareness and help direct energy for cultivation purposes.

At the physical level, you can enjoy excellent health by practicing the Eight Treasures and at the same time you can increase your longevity. Too many people today feel they don't even want to live long because they fear the debilitation of old age. The Eight Treasures help you become and remain healthy in old age. Modern scientists have ascertained that the chronobiological potential of a healthy human lasts 120 years. Using the Eight Treasures, many practitioners have achieved at least this life span in a healthy condition. This result may be possible for those who engage in diligent lifetime practice. Certainly anyone can become healthier and happier.

By practicing these energy-guiding exercises, you can unblock and relieve energy congestion in the body and gradually eliminate the stress that has accumulated over the course of time. You may also redirect the flow of vitality so that every muscle, nerve and organ is nourished and tonified.

At the mental level, you can sharpen your mental capacity and reactivate dormant components in the body (such as the nervous system and spinal cord) which directly affect the mind. With sharpened intellect and a clear mind, you can learn more efficiently.

By practicing the Eight Treasures, you can also enhance the

depth of your spirituality, which contains the potential to become one with the universe, to reflect its depth, and to know everything through non-knowing.

The Eight Treasures were developed and conceived in our tradition specifically as a foundational exercise, a stepping stone upon which many other exercises can be built. They are a valuable practice for everybody, whether you want to enjoy them for basic health benefits or go on to explore their higher levels for further development and refinement of your full life potential.

Make the Eight Treasures Your Lifetime Practice

A Commentary by Hua-Ching Ni

Whatever you learn, you need to develop yourself. If you do not develop yourself, and you learn 100 styles of martial arts, what will you become? You become scattered, and you have attained nothing. If you learn one good system and keep practicing it, then after some years you can really develop from that practice.

Martial art and *t'ai chi* teachers have reasons for requiring you to do certain things. It is training for your personal growth. However, no matter what system you learn, eventually you still need to attune or adjust it to yourself. Ask yourself, does it fit me? Sometimes by doing it a little differently, you can adjust it to make yourself feel good. That is more important than rigidly following the form.

Do not be discouraged if you cannot perform the movements very well at the beginning. You will do well later. Do not worry about how you do it or how good it looks. That does not matter. What matters is that you are alive and you can do it! In doing the Eight Treasures, or any kind of exercise, it is important just to keep moving. All movement has a pattern, so focus on the overall pattern rather than on the details of the movement. As you continue the practice, over time, you can refine the details.

When I was a student, I wished I could do the same as the master or be better than the master on the first day. Now, I would say: do not frustrate yourself. In the beginning, do whatever you can do and feel happy about it.

The Eight Treasures can also be used as a preparation for meditation and to restore normalcy after meditation. However, you should allow some time before the quiet sitting and after the gentle movement for natural adjustment of the body's energy. The adjustment happens by itself; the mind does not need to do anything.

I need to make a very important point. This *dao-in* movement does not require great force. If you use too much strength, as martial arts do, it will tighten the body too much. Forceful practice does not allow the energy channels to function naturally on their own. Each channel has a different number of points. You do not need to pay specific attention to them unless you feel soreness in the muscle. That tells you that there is a corresponding problem, which usually requires no specific attention, because doing your regular practice will help encourage natural recovery. That is the special value of these movements.

I have seen many people who achieved highly in martial arts and could stand up against several opponents. However, that type of excellence is not valued by a serious student of immortal practice. A wise student knows that not everyone needs to be an excellent fighter, yet everyone's body needs to be healthy. People might be good fighters, but they may neglect their overall health.

A few suggestions for you: when you exercise, do not take off any clothing during the movements. Instead, remove excess clothes at the beginning. You already know how much clothing you need to protect yourself. Particularly, do not take off any clothes after you warm up. That will invite a virus. Once you start moving, you feel hot, but the heat will slowly decrease. Many *t'ai chi* practitioners may have some trouble for a long time because of this, but don't take clothes off while or after exercising, only before.

Also, keep your back as upright as possible, without being stiff. Don't suddenly stretch your leg or any other part of your body. You have to give yourself time to warm up, then you can stretch.

Q: I saw one of the mentors demonstrating the Eight Treasures; and the way he does it is a little different than I've seen before.

Master Ni: Yes, you will also observe me doing it a little differently, and my sons doing it a little differently. This is natural. As in writing Chinese calligraphy, if you imitate exactly what I do, even after you are developed, it will be similar but hardly the same. I allow all students to be a little different, depending upon their achievement and depending on what energy they display. The reason we put the practice on a video is to establish a general standard for the movements.

Q: Can each of the Eight Treasures be isolated and done alone, or can they be done in various sequences?

Master Ni: You should follow the given sequence, you can do an isolated movement for a specific purpose. For example, you might specifically need to do something to adjust yourself if you have been sitting too much, walking too long, or lying down too long. In that case, you can do a simple movement without doing the whole sequence. Always relax between movements.

Q: Are the two most important principles first to follow the movements, and second to follow the breathing?

Master Ni: First learn the general movements, then come to the details later. That will be better. If you pay too much attention to the breathing and all the details at the beginning, it will slow you down so much that you might lose interest in doing it at all.

You will eventually need to learn to control the breath. You cannot control your inhaling and exhaling that well in the beginning, but as you continue, your control will improve. Breathing is like pouring water in a big teapot. Inhale until the pot is full, regulating the flow so that the water comes in evenly. When full, put the lid on it, keeping it full for a short while. Then you slowly let the water out of the teapot, at the same slow speed. It is like pumping air into your body. If you talk, then there is no air being pumped in.

Q: When you do this, should you concentrate on any part of the body, like the spine?

Master Ni: In the first stage, do not focus your attention on any particular internal or external spot until the awareness comes naturally, otherwise you will distract yourself from learning the movements themselves. It is the same when you learn *t'ai chi* movement; at the beginning you do not learn the breathing and everything else, you simply learn the movements and slowly add the details.

When doing the Eight Treasures, we pay attention to the movements and arrange the flow of our bodily energy, or *chi*. Do your fingers feel warm after you have done the movements? If your fingers do not warm up, it often means that your physical energy is low. If you constantly work on it, it will improve. When you get older, the inner organs drop down, but doing this movement brings them up again. We use the Eight Treasures to learn how to adjust the condition of our physical structure, muscles and nervous system. So we do them for external and internal benefit.

Q: Should all of the movements come from the tan tien?

Master Ni: The practice does correspond to the three *tan tien*. Any movement that comes from the spine to the brain is reflected to the internal organ systems and to the three *tan tien*. However, it is not suitable to overemphasize one position. For example, martial artists overemphasize the lower *tan tien* to maintain balance and strength for fighting.

Of course, if you do any movement you have to center yourself well. You must prevent yourself from falling! The Eight Treasures provides balance and helps you develop all three *tan tien* in a unified way.

Any movement we do, and even any sound we hear, stimulates and affects the brain. The brain is the root of your physical being. A healthy brain is reflected in the internal organs, which receive the benefit. The fingers are also connected with the internal organs. You can learn these details as you develop your practice further.

Q: I live in the southern hemisphere. Should I face north when I do the Eight Treasures? Most books I read say to face south.

Master Ni: Yes. However, I think east is best. East always represents life energy. No matter where you are, it is a standard direction.

Q: Is it best to do the exercise in the morning?

Master Ni: I always feel that the morning hours are golden. You can do it in the afternoon or early evening. However, if you do it in the evening, and if you pump too much energy inside yourself, then it will be hard for you to fall asleep; then, the next morning you will oversleep and feel bad about it. The best time to do it is around or before sunrise. It may be difficult to get up so early, but give it a try.

In ancient times, people worshiped the sun, the moon and the stars. The golden light of the sun resembles our immortal soul and the moon's brightness resembles the brightness of the mind. The Big Dipper symbolizes the spirits of one's life being and the mentality of the individual. Now we are much more intellectual and the scope of our knowledge is greater, but we must still develop our energy to strengthen our life spirit and support our mental abilities.

Q: Master Ni, I have been doing the Eight Treasures for a few months now, and I would really like to share it with others.

Master Ni: Just doing it for yourself is most beneficial. However, if you wish to become a teacher, I would like you to learn it better, and know more about how energy flows. Let your development happen naturally.

Whenever you learn something and think about teaching it, you must ask, "Does it serve me or not?" If it does not serve or help you, and you teach it, it will never serve anybody you teach, either. Therefore, be sure that you understand it very well.

To teach the Eight Treasures, you must first contact the Universal Society of the Integral Way, register as a Mentor and be certified to teach. There is a form at the back of this book which you can use to request more information about this.

Section 2
Beginning Practice

At the beginning level, the focus is primarily on learning the sequence of movements, improving your coordination, strength, flexibility and stamina, improving health or resolving health problems, becoming comfortable with doing physical exercise and attaining consistency in practice. Thus you control and guide your energy for better support of your body, mind and spirit.

Bringing the Sea to the Top of the Mountain
(Figure 2)

Chapter 2

Beginning Your Practice

1
Learning from This Book

This book is designed to be used together with the videotape *The Eight Treasures*™ (VHS) available from SevenStar Communications. The key to learning is consistent practice, which means regular repetition of the exercise. After you learn the movements from watching the videotape, it may be helpful to practice in front of a mirror to check yourself.

Classes and special seminars are also available through the Universal Society of the Integral Way. Mentors of the USIW teach classes in different parts of the United States and many other countries in the world. You may contact the College of Tao or the USIW for a list of currently registered Mentors in your area by using the form at the back of this book.

2
Practicing the Eight Treasures

Practicing the Eight Treasures is not merely external. In a way, practicing the Eight Treasures is like reading a book. The external aspect of reading the book causes an internal response. When you practice Eight Treasures, your external physical movement causes a corresponding internal energy movement. You move and align your energy when you practice, yet the internal energy continues moving after you have finished practicing. During the few minutes after you practice, when you rest, the energy will continue to flow strongly through the energy channels.

You can gain a better understanding of these energy movements from the descriptions of the body's energy channels. There are twelve basic channels that relate to the organ systems of the body. There are also eight extraordinary channels, discussed further below. Channels are sometimes called "meridians," but the word channel better describes their function.

The movements of the Eight Treasures connect with the twelve main channels, along with the eight extraordinary channels which are reservoirs for accumulated energy or *chi*. The main *yang* energy channel is called the Governing or *Du* channel, and it runs from the perineum up the spine and over the top of the head to below the nose. The main *yin* energy channel is called the Conception or *Ren* channel; it runs from the perineum up the center front of the body to approximately below the nose. This is why the tongue is placed on the roof of the mouth during the Eight Treasures or any *chi* exercise, to connect these two main *yin* and *yang* channels.

When you do the Eight Treasures, all twelve basic channels, plus the Governing (*Du*) and Conception (*Ren*) channels, work together to attain the normal function of each. In other words, each movement connects with all of the energy channels. This is how you can attain good health from doing the movements.

The Eight Treasures are not hard to understand. Some energy from below moves upward, some energy moves from right to left, from left to right and from the center to both sides. There is both horizontal and vertical expansion. There is expansion on the left side, right side, front and back. The energy moves in all directions. This is one of the reasons why the Eight Treasures serve as a foundation for learning *t'ai chi*.

After you learn the basic movements, then you can benefit from learning the channels and points associated with each movement and focusing on them as you exercise. They are discussed in more detail in the advanced sections of this book. It is good to understand a little about energy circulation, and know how your practice improves the circulation of *chi* in your body and brain.

The *yang* channels are in back, or outside; the *yin* channels are in front, or inside.

There are six "hand" channels; three of these are *yin* channels on the inside of the arms, and three are *yang* channels on the outside of the arms. The three *yin* channels flow from the chest down the inside of the arms to the fingertips. The three *yang* channels flow from the fingertips up the back of the arms, across the shoulders to the face and head.

Correspondingly, there are six "foot" channels. Three *yin* channels flow from the inside of the feet and legs upward to the abdomen. Three *yang* channels flow down from the back along the outside of the legs to the toes.

Each time you move your *yin* channels, the *yang* channels run. Each time you move your *yang* channels, the *yin* channels run. So *yin* follows *yang*, and *yang* follows *yin*. They are never separate from each other. Therefore, the ancient instruction is:

"When one channel moves, all channels move. When one channel rests, all channels rest or slow down." Using this principle, you can use the movements to develop an understanding of the universal law of movement.

3
Practical Guidelines

Guidelines for Approaching Practice

Clothing: Clothing should be loose and comfortable. Cotton is best because it is natural and allows the skin to "breathe." Shoes with thin, flat soles are good because they allow better contact between the soles of your feet and the ground. Adjust the layers of clothing before you warm up; do not remove clothing after you warm up, or during the practice.

Place: Preferably outdoors or in a place with good air circulation. Try to select a place outside where there is a lot of fresh air among the trees. Never practice the Eight Treasures in a damp environment, or in very humid or bad weather.

Do not practice above the fourth floor of a building, because the electromagnetic energy field is considerably weaker and less conducive to effective practice. In the Eight Treasures, you connect with the earth's energy as well as the energy of the upper sphere of Heaven, and the lower sphere of bodily life.

Time: The best time to practice the Eight Treasures is at sunrise. Other good times are 5:00 to 7:00 a.m., and 5:00 to 7:00 p.m. Any other time is acceptable except noon when the *yang* energy is too strong. (If you do it in the evening, be especially careful to avoid collecting too much energy in the head.)

Generally, it is suitable to do the entire practice in the morning. In the late evening, it is not suitable to do the first four treasures, because if you overdo them, you will over-stimulate your brain right before you go to sleep. The evening is a time when you should keep your energy down so you can have a peaceful sleep. However, people who have trouble sleeping may find that the seventh and eighth treasures are very helpful.

Direction: East is always a good direction to face. South is good if you live in the northern hemisphere and north if you live in the southern hemisphere. However, for practical purposes, if you practice indoors and fresh air is coming from an open window located in the east, face east.

Avoid: Practicing in damp areas, during disturbing weather conditions (storms, hurricanes), with a full stomach, when emotionally disturbed with lots of negative thoughts, or when so sick that rest is more beneficial. Women should not practice during times of heavy menstrual flow. Avoid eating one hour before and one-half hour after practice, because the digestion of food draws too much energy to the stomach area.

Repetition: In general, beginners may perform 12, 9, 7 or a minimum of 5 repetitions of each motion within the movements. Advanced practitioners may do 3 times and work toward doing only one repetition to allow time for other cultivation exercises.

Breathing: The breath should be gentle, relaxed, smooth and even. This will bring your breathing low and deep. In most movements it is better if the breath is slow and long. Breath should also be continuous. Do not hold your breath, except during part of one movement in the eighth treasure (8.F: White Crane Stretches Its Legs Behind and Forward). You may do several cycles of breath in a particular position. The important part is that the breath be relaxed and natural.

Trust your body. This is not a purely physical practice nor is it a mental practice. It is a practice of unification. Try not to think too much. Keep your mind calm and relaxed, and watch what it wants to do. Allow the movements to develop in a natural manner.

Also keep your body calm and relaxed. Whenever you are tense, your *chi* becomes blocked or stagnant. Two common areas of tension are the lower back and shoulders, although people tend to tense up in all areas of the body. The Eight Treasures will help open up such blockages and make you more flexible. Therefore, it is important to remain open and relaxed, so your joints are flexed, the organs are internally massaged and the *chi* can flow in your energy channels.

If you are learning in a class, your instructor can offer a helpful perspective on your progress and may be able to work with you individually. He or she will review your progress at several stages along the way.

Flexibility in learning and practicing the Eight Treasures: The outward movements and details of the Eight Treasures are useful tools for learning and practice. However, the essence of the Eight Treasures is the energy flow that it induces and guides. Outward variations in the movements will inevitably occur, reflecting different styles, personal energetic expressions, or different times and places.

This book and the videotape present a standard teaching form of the Eight Treasures to assist initial learning and communication, but are not meant to imply that this is the only "correct" way to perform the Eight Treasures. Different variations presented in this book or the videotape, or outside of the standard teaching form, are possible and valid. Understanding the basic principles will help you teach yourself as you progress. Flexibility in developing and following the form's essence is the key.

Don't become overwhelmed.
Be patient with yourself; don't try to learn everything at once. Learn a little at a time and you will do it well with no difficulty. After learning the first few movements, you will discover that learning other movements is faster and easier. Soon you will discover their ease and simplicity.

Have fun!
Most people feel very relaxed and calm after practicing the Eight Treasures. If you can smile while you are engaging in the movements, then you are probably physically relaxed too. Maintain a positive attitude; this also helps you cultivate positive energy with the movements. Enjoy learning!

Guidelines for Learning

1. Learn the movements in sequence.

2. At first, learn the movements in general. Don't think too much or get caught up in small details in the beginning. Experience the

natural movements of your body. Refinement comes with consistent practice.

3. Do not be concerned with the breathing patterns until later. The breathing should be slow, deep, and natural.

4. Perform the movements without strain or pain according to your physical state. If any part of a movement hurts, you are pushing too far or straining, doing the movement incorrectly. If you have a physical limitation, you may need to adapt the movement.

5. It is more beneficial to do the movements slowly. This way, you stay more relaxed, you can focus more on each part of each movement and avoid making inadvertent mistakes.

6. Consistent practice builds strength and stamina and creates internal balance and harmony.

7. Be relaxed. When you relax and go slowly, you move better and the breath naturally synchronizes with your movements.

Guidelines for Further Refinement

1. Relax the muscles of the whole body. Do not use stiff strength.

2. Free your mind from other thoughts to focus on the movements.

3. Work toward enlarging the upward and downward movements of your diaphragm. This reinforces the contraction of the abdominal muscles and benefits the internal organs.

4. Touch the tip of the tongue to the upper palate throughout the exercises.

5. Do not use fans in hot weather. Also avoid cold showers, baths or swimming immediately after exercising.

6. Avoid food or drink for 30 minutes after exercising.

7. Do not sit or lie down immediately after the exercise. It is beneficial to walk at least 200 steps even if indoors.

8. Do not practice after using alcohol, drugs, tobacco or stimulants.

9. Women should avoid practice during the heavy flow of the menstrual period.

10. Don't judge yourself or your progress. People progress at different speeds during different stages of the practice.

4
Stances

Several stances are used in starting or performing the Eight Treasures. These are "feet shoulder-width apart," "feet together," "heels together," "bow stance," "horse stance," and "cat stance."

For "feet shoulder-width apart," the feet are parallel and spaced with the heels about the same distance apart as the shoulders are wide. Ideally, the feet are parallel, not "spread eagled" (toes pointing apart) or "pigeon toed" (toes pointing together). However, they may not be perfectly parallel if this would be uncomfortable or require straining. Figure 3 shows the foot positions for "feet shoulder-width apart."

Figure 3
Feet Shoulder-Width
Apart Foot Position

Figure 4
Feet Together
Foot Position

For "feet together," the feet are positioned next to each other so they are touching on the inside edges. However, they may have some space between them if you would otherwise be unstable or lose balance when moving. Figure 4 shows the foot positions for "feet together."

For "heels together," the heels are together and touching, with the forward parts of the feet separated at an angle. Figure 5 shows the foot positions for "heels together."

Figure 5
Heels Together
Foot Position

Figure 6
Bow Stance

In the "bow stance" (Figure 6), one foot is forward (the forward foot) at a 45-degree angle from the other foot (the back foot) into a moderately wide stance. The weight is shifted forward so that the forward knee is bent and over the toes, and the back is straight without leaning forward. The toes of the forward foot point in the direction of the leg, while the toes of the back foot are about a 45-degree angle to the side. The heels of the forward and back feet are slightly apart on opposite sides of the line made by the direction of the forward leg. The back leg is straight, but not locked. In a "left bow stance," the left foot is forward (See Figures 6 and 7), and in a "right bow stance," the right foot is forward.

Figure 7
Bow Stance
Foot Position

In the "horse stance," the feet are spaced wide apart and you sit low, as though astride a horse. The feet are spaced about three times shoulder-width apart, and ideally are parallel. The hips are

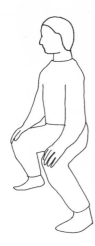

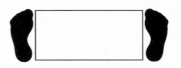

tucked slightly forward, so that the back is straight. The lower legs are vertical or close to vertical, and the upper legs are horizontal

Figure 9
Horse Stance Foot Position

or close to horizontal. Figures 8 and 9 show the body and foot positions for the "horse stance."

Figure 8
Horse Stance

In the "cat stance," the forward foot in a bow stance has been brought straight back about half way, with its toes touching the ground and the back leg fully weighted. In a "left cat stance" the left foot is forward (Figure 10), and in a "right cat stance" the right foot is forward. Figure 10 shows the foot positions for a "left cat stance."

Figure 10
Cat Stance
Foot Position

5
Enjoy Learning

Enjoy the Eight Treasures as pleasant, gentle movement that rewards you with greater health and happiness! It is important to do all the movements from the beginning to the end, but they can also be done individually if you need to emphasize one specific movement.

The Eight Treasures is a wonderful *dao-in*, an effective re-alignment of your natural rhythm. You do not have to be in excellent athletic condition to do Eight Treasures. It is gentle and simple. Complex movements are not necessary for improving your health and supporting your self-development.

6
The Health Aspects of Each Treasure

As a whole, the movements of the Eight Treasures continuously align the whole body. In addition, each treasure has its specific benefits.

The first treasure, *Sustaining Heaven with Both Hands to Adjust the Three Warmers*, benefits the following organ systems:

- Respiratory System
- Endocrine System
- Digestive System
- Elimination System

The second treasure, *Drawing the Bow with Both Hands to Aim at a Distant Target*, benefits the following:

- Cerebral System
- Spinal System
- Tendo-muscular System
- Immune System
- Heart/Lung Systems

The third treasure, *Raising the Hands to Adjust the Stomach and Spleen*, benefits the following:

- Digestive System
- Elimination System
- Metabolism

The fourth treasure, *Turning the Head to Tonify the Nervous System*, very specifically:

- tonifies the spine, spinal cord and skeletal structure

The fifth treasure, *Swaying the Spinal Column to Take Away Heart Fire*, benefits the following:

- Digestive System
- Elimination System

The sixth treasure, *Raising the Heels to Remove Physical and Mental Weakness*, benefits the following:

- Cerebral/Spinal System
- Abdominal Viscera

The seventh treasure, *Tightening the Tendons to Reinforce Yourself*, benefits the body by tightening up:

- Tendo-muscular System
- Nervous System

The eighth treasure, *Grabbing the Ankles to Strengthen Your Vital Force*, benefits the following organ systems:

- Endocrine System
- Bones and Tendons
- Digestion and Elimination Systems
- Cerebral/Spinal Systems

7
Questions and Answers

Q: How often should I practice?

A: Like any form of exercise, it is important to proceed gradually, especially if you are not accustomed to daily exercise. It is never advisable to overdo any exercise program. Only do a reasonable amount; this means the amount to which your body can comfortably adapt. Your strength is built up by regular consistent exercise rather than excessive or infrequent periods of practice. Make exercise a part of your balanced daily life.

Q: How important is breathing, and how should I breathe?

A: As in all exercise, your breath is of great importance. Breathe through the nose, slowly and deeply, taking a full breath that extends down to the abdomen. Modern people tend to breathe in a shallow manner, in the upper part of the lungs only, but deep breathing will enhance the quality of your health and increase the spiritual nature of the exercise. Keep your breath slow, steady and even, and coordinate your movements with your breath.

Some martial arts practitioners emphasize unusual or special breathing techniques. However, such techniques are not advisable for your Eight Treasures practice. Keep your breathing normal and enjoy your natural, healthy self-development.

Q: What should I think about when exercising?

A: You need to concentrate on what you are doing and on your breath. Your practice will be more effective if you can keep your mind from wandering to other things. As you make the animal motions of a lion or tiger, for example, it is also effective to visualize or imagine yourself as the animal. This will help you understand and perform the movements well.

Q: What if some of the exercises are too hard for me? Should I skip them?

A: If you cannot do a movement as it is described, try to build up to it by practicing it in a way that is not too strenuous for you.

Q: If I get out of breath or breathe rapidly, does that mean I should only do one or two sections of the Eight Treasures at a time, or just go very slowly? I'm not very good at exercise.

A: Yes, keep practicing just one section at a time until your body becomes accustomed to it. All students should practice at a slow speed to learn more thoroughly.

Q: I'm a little out of shape. I can't do the exercises nearly as well as you do in the videotape or even as well as the Mentor who is teaching me. Actually, I am starting to do this exercise a little late in life so I do not have as much flexibility, etc. Will I still experience the movement of chi?

A: Regardless of your age, with consistent practice you can benefit from the full potential of Eight Treasures. There have been many examples of healthy, long-living people who spent the first half of their life struggling with illness until they began to engage in *chi* practice. At the same time, we don't want to encourage younger students to delay their practice.

Q: Should I do the Eight Treasures if I have a slight cold or am feeling a little tired?

A: Yes, although more conservatively and without overexpanding your *chi*. Generally, you will feel better after mobilizing your *chi* toward a constructive use. You may be able to use the practice to ward off illness, and to re-energize yourself. It also depends upon the circumstances. You need to apply your awareness and good common sense.

Q: Sometimes when I start to do the Eight Treasures, I cannot concentrate very well. Should I still do them?

A: Yes, do not give up. You can start with one or two movements within a section first and repeat them until your mind becomes more in concert with your body.

Here are some other suggestions that may help. (1) Stand calmly for a minute or two before you begin practice; you can use this time to relax and breathe calmly from the lower abdomen. (2) As you practice, mentally focus on your body and the physical movements. (3) Pay attention to how the movements feel, your posture, and whether you have any tense areas to loosen up and relax. (4) If you find that your mind is busy trying to keep track of things you need to do, get in the habit of making reminder lists or using a calendar system, so you can clear your mind for practice.

Q: My schedule is irregular. If I only do Eight Treasures once a week, will I still be benefitted by it?

A: Yes; however, even during a fifteen-minute break, you can still find a way to practice parts of the Eight Treasures on a daily basis.

Q: When I do the rotation of the knee joints in the warm-up exercises and The Weeping Willow Shivers in the Early Morning Breeze, my knees make a lot of cracking noises. It's a little embarrassing. Is that all right? What causes that?

A: It means excess toxin buildup in the joints and may signify arthritis later in life. However, after practicing for a while, the noise in the joints should diminish in proportion to the benefits generated from practice. The movement will clear out the buildup of toxins in the joints, so don't worry about the noises.

Q: In the same exercise (Weeping Willow), we do several neck rolls. Once somebody told me that it was not good to do that. Is it safe?

A: One needs to engage in this movement very gently, carefully and slowly so as not to cause any injury from abrupt or forced motion of the neck. In general, this is no concern unless a person has severe neck spurs. The problem with the way most people do neck rolls is that they turn the neck by using the neck muscles, which not only tenses those muscles but also places pressure on the neck joints. The correct motion in this movement is not really a "neck roll;" instead, you tilt the upper body slightly while allowing the neck to be fully relaxed, so the head follows gravity and gently rolls in the circles. Therefore the neck muscles are not used, they are actually relaxed and feel better afterward, and the neck joints are made more flexible without damage.

When in doubt, it is always a good idea to consult your physician before beginning any exercise program.

Q: How precisely do I have to follow the movements?

A: It is important to understand the principle of flexibility in doing these exercises. It is also an important spiritual principle.

The Eight Treasures is not a rigid exercise. Be flexible as you proceed with your practice. The material in this book is presented as a guideline, not a command or a strict regimen. Especially as you become more familiar with the exercises, let your body tell you, for example, how many repetitions of any movement you do. For example, if your shoulders are sore or tight, you may wish to do a few extra repetitions of certain movements or sections. Let the exercises become a means of communication between your body, mind and spirit.

You can do each movement a different number of times for different purposes or to suit your convenience. For instance, beginners might imitate the videotape for the purposes of simplicity. At other times we need to practice one movement more than another or we can feel the benefits from some movements more quickly and easily than with another. Therefore, you can adjust your practice according to your needs.

These guidelines on the significance of certain numbers come from the ancient tradition that values and integrates mysticism and mathematics. They are a good guide for our practice. Here is the numerology related to the number of repetitions in any of the treasures:

3, 5, 7   good numbers for repetitions
  3   Heaven, Earth, and Man / *shen, jing,* and *chi*
  5   five elemental organs
  7   seven energy centers
  9   nine palaces in the body
 12   twelve channels or twelve organs/systems
 27   derived from nine; nine times three (three spheres of being)
 36   nine times four (four directions, seasons and extremities)

Differences between this book and the videotape

At first glance, some differences may be found between the movement descriptions in this book and as performed on the accompanying videotape. However, nearly all apparent differences are only expressions of the possible range of acceptable variation in performing the movements. In a few cases, there are some small inconsistencies in the videotape, as noted in the sections below. In the important aspects, however, the videotape presents a standard for performing the movements. The descriptions in this book give more detailed and precise information to assist in learning the standard form within the range of acceptable variations. The breathing descriptions tend to be more precise in the book. Also, the movement descriptions in the book consistently start on the left side, while most, but not all, movements on the videotape are mirrored, starting on the right side.

Alternative Ways of Performing Portions of the Movements

The alternatives listed in this book tend to be adaptations of particular movements that can be made to accommodate particular physical needs or levels of ability. Individual variations in performing portions of the movements that do not affect their essential nature can also be seen in the videotape. Many individual variations are possible and can be expected.

Breathing During the Eight Treasures

Most of the breathing instructions for performing the Eight Treasures can be summarized as: Inhale during upward and inward movements, and exhale during downward and outward movements. Breathing during certain portions of the movements, such as those which are upward and outward, or transitional movements, requires specific instructions as given in the videotape. The breathing instructions in the videotape and this book are intended to be consistent, and should vary only to the extent that some of the breathing instructions on the videotape are not always exactly synchronized with the movements.

Starting Movements on the Left Side

Generally, it is best to start movements on the left (*yang*) side, although they may be started on the right (*yin*) side for balance or energy adjustment. In the Eight Treasures videotape, most movements are shown starting on the right side. This was done to present a "mirror image" of each movement, making it easier to follow along with the videotape, reversing the sides. However, several movements on the videotape are shown starting on the left side, so they do not present a "mirror image" and, ideally, would be done as shown, without reversing the sides. These movements are 7.B: The Tiger Grabs Its Prey, portions of 7.C: Clench The Teeth, Widen The Eyes, And Strike To The Four Directions, 8.A: The White Crane Washes Its Wing Feathers, 8.B: The White Crane Turns Its Head To Look Up, 8.C: The White Crane Twists Its Body To Look Up, 8.D: The White Crane Sharpens Its Beak, and 8.G: The White Crane Guards The Plum Flower.

Clench the Teeth, Widen the Eyes, and Strike to the Four Directions

In the movement Clench the Teeth, Widen the Eyes, and Strike to the Four Directions, the videotape is slightly inconsistent. As described in this book, the sequence should generally consist of single strikes with left and right fists to the front, sets of double strikes with left and right fists to the front, single strikes with left and right fists to alternate sides, and single strikes with left and right fists to the front to finish. One or more gathers should be done before each strike or set of strikes. The pairs of left and right single strikes to the front or to alternate sides, or the pairs of left and right sets of double strikes to the front, are usually done as *pairs* (begin with the left strike or set of strikes), and may be repeated before continuing with the next pair of strikes or sets of strikes.

Chapter 3

Learning the Movements

This written description of the Eight Treasures™ is designed to be used together with the companion videotape. Only the basics of the movements are described here. For further proficiency, students may take classes with a registered instructor of the Universal Society of the Integral Way (information is available at the back of this book).

This chapter describes only the beginning level. Information for intermediate and advanced practice is provided in later chapters of this book.

Warm-Up

The Warm-Up is very important prior to starting the Eight Treasures movements, because it activates the flow of *chi* in all parts of the body, and is also good for relieving stress. The Warm-Up may also be done by itself to promote energy circulation at any time during the day.

The Warm-Up starts in the *tan tien*. "*Tan tien*" is the term for the energy centers of the body. The lower *tan tien* is located in the abdomen, about two inches below the navel. It is very important in the Eight Treasures, and when you see a reference in this book to "*tan tien*" it means the lower *tan tien* unless indicated otherwise. Also of some importance are the middle *tan tien*, located at the "heart center" or in the center of the chest, and the upper *tan tien* between the eyebrows.

The Warm-Up also focuses on the kidney area, slightly above the waist on both sides of the spine.

1. Awakening *Chi* in the Channels

These warm-up movements help to awaken or activate *chi* in the energy channels of the body.

1.A Tapping the trunk

Start with the feet shoulder-width apart. Let your arms hang down at the sides of the body. Relax your body, especially the neck and shoulder muscles. Initiate a turning movement by shifting your weight from side to side, turning at the waist and pelvic area to cause your arms to swing. With loose fists, gently tap the area below your waist (slightly below the level of your navel) in front and back, which is called the lower *tan tien*. The gentle weight shift or rocking from side to side helps give momentum to your arm swings.

Continue tapping the trunk lightly, gradually moving the fists up the chest in a "V" pattern to your shoulders.

Gradually backtrack down the same path, returning to the lower *tan tien*. Repeat a few times.

BREATHING: Breathe deeply and naturally.

1.B Tapping the trunk and arms

Start with the feet shoulder-width apart. Make a loose fist with the right hand, lift and extend the left arm, and tap from the level of the navel to under the arm, up the shoulder to the neck, down the shoulder, down the inside of the arm to the palm, back up the outside of the arm, and in along the shoulder to the neck.

Repeat on the other side with the left hand and right arm.

BREATHING: Breathe deeply and naturally.

1.C Tapping the back and legs

Start with the feet wide apart (the width of the horse stance, but with legs straight). Making loose fists with the hands, bend forward at the waist and tap with the backs of the fists in circles over the kidneys, moving up the spine, out to the sides, down the sides, and back in to the spine, circling a few times.

Continue tapping with the insides of the fists along the sides of the buttocks, down the outside of the legs to the ankles, switch to the inside of the ankles and tap up the inside of the legs to the connection of the legs to the trunk (the ligaments on each side of the crotch).

Bring the feet in to shoulder-width apart, and tap with the inside of loose fists against the connection of the legs to the trunk, alternating with legs straight and legs bent a few times, giving an up and down motion while tapping.

BREATHING: Deep and natural.

1.D Swinging the arms back and jumping up

Start with feet shoulder-width apart. Freely swing the arms from front to back until you find the point of natural resistance in back, and then let them swing to the front again.

After several swings, to enhance the movement, bend the knees slightly and lift the heels as the arms swing back and up.

After several more swings, jump up as the arms swing back and up. Feel as though the momentum of your arms swinging back carries you up. Repeat, going progressively higher each time.

Then, gradually jump less and less high, slow down and gradually stop swinging the arms, bending the knees and lifting the heels, and return to a normal standing position.

BREATHING: Inhale when arms swing back and up.

2. Loosening and opening up the joints

These warm-up movements loosen and open up the major joints of the body, allowing *chi* to pass through them more easily. They include the three parts of the Fourth Treasure called "The Weeping Willow Shivers in the Early Morning Breeze." When done as part of the Eight Treasures, these movements work with the *chi* in your channels and therefore have more specific benefits, as described later. Several optional movements are also included in the Warm-Up to open up the remaining joints of the body.

2.A Turning the neck

Start with heels together and hands together. Men place right hand underneath left hand, women place left hand underneath right hand. Place the thumb of the upper hand inside the thumb of the lower hand, and the first joint of one of the fingers of the upper hand over the side of the big knuckle of the little finger on the lower hand.

Keeping the neck relaxed, slightly bend the upper body and shoulders to allow gravity to roll the head gently and slowly to the left, back to the right, and front in a circle, repeating several times.

Reverse direction when the head is bent forward, and repeat.

BREATHING: Inhale as your head circles to the back, exhale as it circles to the front.

2.B (optional) Turning the shoulders

Keeping the arms relaxed, lift the left shoulder and turn the waist to roll the shoulder from front to back, repeating a few times. Reverse, lifting the shoulder back to front, repeating a few more times.

Repeat on the other side.

NOTE: As an alternative, big shoulder rotations can be done. Lift the arm on the left side straight up above the shoulder and rotate it down in front and up in back, circling a few times. Reverse direction, circling a few more times. Repeat on the other side.

BREATHING: Inhale when circling up and exhale when circling down.

2.C (optional) Turning the elbows
Place the right hand over the elbow area in front of the left arm hanging down at the side. Keeping the hand loosely over the elbow area, bend the left arm up at the elbow, turning it up toward the body on the inside of the right arm, and then circle the left forearm back down away from the body. Repeat a few times.

Reverse direction, bending the left arm at the elbow and turning it up away from the body and back down towards the body to circle inside the right arm.

Repeat on the other side.

BREATHING: Inhale when circling up and exhale when circling down.

2.D (optional) Turning the wrists
Keeping the arms relaxed and hanging down at the sides, turn the hands around the wrist on each side, a few times toward the trunk in front, then reverse for a few more times away from the trunk in front.

Gently shake the hands, then the hands and lower arms, then the hands and lower and upper arms.

NOTE: As an alternative, clasp the hands with fingers interlaced and trace a "figure eight" in front of the body. Try to get a full range of motion when turning and bending the wrists. After repeating a few times, reverse direction for a few more times.

BREATHING: Breathe deeply and naturally.

2.E (optional) Turning the waist
Start with feet wide apart (the width of a horse stance, but with legs straight). Place the hands on the waist on each side, and bend forward at the waist. Keeping the hands in place and turning at the waist, circle the upper body around to the left, lean back, to the right, and bend forward again, repeating a few times. When bent forward, reverse direction and repeat a few more times, then straighten up.

BREATHING: Inhale when circling to the back, exhale when circling to the front.

2.F Turning the hips

Start with heels together, or farther apart if necessary for balance. Place the palms of the hands over the kidneys and rub them a few times to warm them up.

Keeping the palms over the kidneys, and the head upright and over the feet, push the hips forward, then to the left, back, to the right, and forward to make a complete rotation. Repeat several times.

Reverse direction and repeat several more times in the opposite direction, then straighten up.

BREATHING: Exhale as the hips circle forward, inhale back.

2.G Turning the knees

Start with feet together. Bend forward at the waist and rest the hands on the knees. Lightly rub the knees to warm them. Make a circle by bending the knees to the left, then in front and to the right, and then straighten them. Repeat several times. Reverse the direction of the circles and repeat several more times.

Next, make circles by bending the knees forward and separating them, moving them out to each side, and circling back as you straighten them. Repeat several more times.

Reverse the direction of the circles and repeat.

BREATHING: Exhale when knees bend down, inhale when straightening up.

2.H Turning the ankles

Lift the left foot. Rotate it at the ankle several times in one direction, then in the other. Alternate pointing and flexing the foot, then shake it to loosen the ankle joint. Repeat for the other foot.

NOTE: An alternative to loosen the ankle joint is to place the left foot at an angle behind you, ball of the foot on the ground and heel in the air. Turn that foot's ankle in big circles, then reverse the direction of the circles. Repeat on the other side.

BREATHING: Deep and natural.

The Eight Treasures Movements

How to practice the Eight Treasures

• Whenever you bend forward or squat, stand up slowly to avoid becoming dizzy.

• Shift the weight from one foot to the other evenly, smoothly and continuously.

• Practicing slowly is more beneficial than going fast. Stay relaxed. However, do not allow the movements to become weak or empty. Staying relaxed while guiding your *chi* through the movements will loosen tension and open blockages.

• Generally keep your spine straight. Never arch your lower back (unless the movement specifically has you doing so). Most people carry tension in the lower back which manifests as arching it. This stresses the area and causes pain over time. It is very important to loosen up and relax the lower back.

• Keep your shoulders relaxed. Make sure that even when your arms rise, the shoulders do not go up. Again, many people carry tension in the neck and shoulders and feel resulting pain in those muscles, so be sure to relax the neck and shoulders.

• Check how you feel as you practice to see if you are still carrying tension in any area. The many benefits of the Eight Treasures include stress and tension reduction. Regular practice will enable you to move (and carry on other aspects of your life) more calmly and purposefully.

• In general, inhale as your arms rise or come in toward the body; and exhale as they descend, or move away from the body.

• Inhaling and exhaling should be soft, even, smooth and continuous. Use the lower abdomen to breathe deeply, fully expanding the lower abdomen to fill the lungs, and fully compressing the lower abdomen to empty the lungs. Keep the shoulders and upper chest relaxed.

• If you start breathing too hard or fast, slow down. Breathing improves with practice.

•Every movement is made up of series of circles, each of which is accompanied by a complete cycle of an inhale and an exhale. Use the breathing instructions to coordinate your breathing with the movements.

•Make sure your spine remains straight unless the movement specifically has bending.

•Feel the movements and focus on what you are doing. You can guide the *chi* with your mind, but do not intellectualize the movements. First get a basic feel for doing the movements. When you start feeling your *chi*, you are ready for the next level.

•Side to start movements on: Generally, it is best to start movements on the left *(yang)* side, although they may be started on the right *(yin)* side for balance or energy adjustment. In the Eight Treasures videotape, most movements are shown starting on the right side. This was done to present a "mirror image" of each movement, making it easier to follow along with the videotape. However, several movements on the videotape are shown starting on the left side, so they do not present a "mirror image" and would ideally be done as shown, without reversing the sides. We prefer to start on the *yang* side because *yang* energy is dynamic and we want to start by moving our energy. The *yin* side follows, as *yang* gives rise to *yin* in the cyclic *t'ai chi* relationship.

•Unless the movement clearly indicates otherwise, each movement may be closed by guiding your energy with your hands to the lower *tan tien*.

1. FIRST TREASURE:
Sustaining Heaven with Both Hands
to Adjust the Three Warmers

Practicing the First Treasure:
•The beak position is formed by putting the tips of the fingers and thumb together in a point.
•Learn to use gentle breathing to guide the body and arms to move.

1.A Move the Stars and Turn the Big Dipper
Start with feet parallel about shoulder-width apart. Form a beak

with the right hand; move the point of the beak, fingers pointing upward, to the base of the spine.

Step forward with your left foot into a "left bow stance." (Left foot steps out approximately 45 degrees, left knee bent, back straight (without leaning forward) and weight shifted forward so the left knee is over the toes. Right leg is straight, but not locked.) As you step, raise your left arm then initiate horizontal circles, circling right and in, left and out (forward), somewhat like lassoing movements, with the left arm at the level (height) of the forehead. This is done by shifting your weight from one leg to another in a rocking motion as your waist turns, thus causing your arm to circle. Make the rocking motion with the weight first transferring to the back leg as the back knee bends and the left arm pulls in, and then pushing the weight forward to the front leg as the arm swings forward again. You are gathering or harvesting energy from the stars, and opening your upper *tan tien*. The motion causes a change from fullness to emptiness and from *yin* to *yang*.

Next make large and round vertical circles. This is done by continuing to shift your weight, but turning the waist only very slightly, and allowing the backward and forward momentum to carry your left arm in big circles in toward your body and down, and away from your body and up. As your left hand comes in and down, it will move from your head down along your body to your lower trunk and then toward the left knee. You are drawing the energy from above, down through your body.

Next, step back with your left foot so your feet are parallel and shoulder-width apart, and gather across the chest. Move your arms out to the left, at the level of the middle *tan tien* (heart center). Make sure you are not raising your shoulders. Slowly, gather or sweep arms across to the right and then back to the left, somewhat like windshield wipers moving parallel to the ground. Each time the leading arm will swing out to be straight as the other hand gathers in toward the middle *tan tien*. Create momentum for these arm movements by shifting your weight slightly and turning the waist from side to side. Repeat several times; you are opening your middle *tan tien* or heart center.

Next, continue gathering from side to side, but bend the knees and make scoops, lowering the left hand and arm from left to right with the back straight, then straightening up as you return from right to left. You are opening your lower *tan tien*. Repeat this several times, progressively bending the knees deeper, then stay low with the knees bent and scoop in both directions in a smaller arc close to the feet.

Still bending forward, bring your
heels together and place your right
hand in the beak shape behind the
tailbone (at the base of the spine) as
you straighten the legs. With your
left hand, make small clockwise
circles in front of your feet.

With your left hand between the
ankles, in a beak shape with fingers
pointing up, slowly straighten up and
continue to raise the left hand from
near the inside of the legs to the front
of the heart center (middle *tan tien*).
Be sure to keep both shoulders
relaxed. As your hand reaches the
heart center, hold the hand still there,
and raise the heels slightly to balance
on the balls of the feet. Be sure your
back is straight and your breathing is
low and relaxed.

Figure 11

Lower your heels, and slightly bend your head to look at your
left hand in the beak shape. Then straighten up and raise your
forearm until your left hand rises in front of your face. Following
the hand with your eyes, turn the "Big Dipper," swinging your left
arm out to the left side, hand still in the beak shape with the fingers
pointing down, and left elbow pointing down to the ground. Continue turning to the left and lift the heels slightly again, so that your
left arm is farther toward the back. Continue looking through the
hole made by the beak (See Figure 11). Still following your hand
with the eyes, lower your heels and return the left hand in front of
the heart center. Repeat several times. This draws the energy from
the earth up through your body.

Conclude by bringing your right hand around in front by the left
hand at the heart center, then lower both hands to guide the energy
to your lower *tan tien* in the abdomen.

Reversing sides, repeat this entire movement on the right side.

BREATHING: Inhale when circling inward during the horizontal
circles, when circling down through the body during the vertical
circles, when gathering inward with the left hand on the first side
(and the right hand, when you reverse sides), when circling inward

in front of the feet, and when moving upward before and during the dippers. Exhale when circling outward during the horizontal circles, when circling back up during the vertical circles, when gathering inward with the opposite hand from the side you started on, when circling outward in front of the feet, when bending forward before the dippers, when moving back downward after each dipper, and when lowering the hands at the end.

1.B The Great Elephant Raises Its Trunk

Start with heels together. Raise the hands slightly to hip level, then bend forward and let the arms swing out to the sides, with the backs of the hands leading, and to the front. Bending at the knees, rock the body in a gentle undulating motion that brings your lower body and then your waist forward. Raise the heels as your body arches forward (see Figure 12). Your hands then "fall" toward the lower *tan tien*, then bring your waist to the back. The hands touch behind the waist, at the small of the back.

Bring the waist forward again, lowering the heels, bending forward at the waist, and allowing the arms again to swing out to the sides and in front. Viewed from the side, your body looks like a wave or an "S" moving from low to high. Move forward and back this way a few times, ending bent forward with the arms in front.

Figure 12

Next, draw the hands back from in front to brush with the backs of the hands across the upper legs, keeping the legs straight. As the hands circle back out and forward, bend the knees so that the hands and knees move forward simultaneously. Repeat several times, brushing further down the upper leg, below the knee and by the ankles on following circles. Finally, assume a full squat with your hands extended in front, then straighten the legs while bending forward, forming beaks with both hands by your ankles. Slowly stand upright, raising your hands near the inside of the legs up to the middle *tan tien* (heart center), then raise the heels. Lower the heels, bend forward slightly at the waist and lower the hands slightly.

Continue, raising the heels and lifting your hands higher (still as beaks, fingers pointing down) to the upper *tan tien* (between the eyebrows). Lower the heels, bend forward slightly at the waist, and lower the hands slightly.

Continue raising the heels and lifting your hands (still as beaks) to the top of your head, and then straight up above your head (as if you were pulling a string). You may look up with the eyes towards your hands to help move your energy upward, but keep the neck straight and unbent. Lower your heels and lower your hands along the "string" until the fingers touch the top of the head. Repeat this, pulling the "string" several times. Conclude by bringing the hands down to the lower abdomen.

BREATHING: In the first part, inhale as the arms come in toward the body and exhale as they move away to the front. In the second part, inhale during upward movements and exhale during downward movements.

1.C The Dolphin's Fins Pat the Water

Start with feet together. Place palms on hips. Guide the hands down the outside of the thighs to the knees, then up the midline with the backs of the hands coming together, along the inside of the thighs and up to the waist, and then back out to the hips. Repeat several times. You are guiding energy up the inside of the thighs, around the waist, and back down the sides of the thighs, in circular motions.

After a few repetitions, when the hands are at their highest, open the feet while keeping the heels together, moving the toes as you bring the hands out to the sides, so the toes point away at 45 degree angles. The hands point forward. Slightly sink by bending the knees, then let yourself "drop," relaxing the knees and letting them bend freely to make a brisk dropping or sitting movement. At the same time, let the arms and hands relax and drop, so the arms are extended straight down, palms facing down

Figure 13

and fingers pointing forward. Let the energy drop instead of push-ing it down.

Pause, then straighten the knees and bring the feet back to-gether. Repeat this part of the movement by guiding the hands back down the outside of the thighs to the knees, back up the insides to the waist, out to the sides as the toes point out, etc. Repeat several times. Be sure that when you drop into the sitting posture, the hips are tucked forward so your lower back is straight (not curved back).

The hands circling up the inside of the legs bring up the water energy, and then pack it into the lower *tan tien*. The hands can be considered "fins," and "patting the water" means bringing the energy to the lower *tan tien*, called the Sea of Elixir.

BREATHING: Inhale with the upward motions, and exhale with the downward motions.

Figure 14

1.D Bringing the Sea to the Top of the Mountain

Start with the heels together. Extend the arms out at the sides and bend forward at the waist. Lower hands near feet, and bring them close together with the wrists crossed and the palms facing up, as if lifting something. Slowly stand up straight, opening your arms and sweeping them up and above your head. Sweep the arms back slightly behind the head, bending gently backward from the waist (see Figure 14), and then allow the arms to fall to each side. Be careful with the back bend; only do what is comfortable. (If your breathing stops or tightens up, then you are bending back too far.) As you become more flexible and stronger, you can bend a little farther back as it becomes comfortable.

Bend forward again to repeat

several times. In this movement, the "top of the mountain" refers to the top of the head, while "the sea" or "reflecting sea" refers to the area between the insides of the two ankles. This movement draws energy from the area of "reflecting sea" up the front of the body to the top of the head.

Straighten and clasp hands behind the head with fingers interlaced. Rise on the balls of the feet (raising the heels) as you pull or flex the elbows back slightly, so your shoulder blades move closer together in your back. Be sure to keep your upper and lower back straight. Lower the heels and relax.

Bend forward slightly and twist the body at the waist to the left, raising the left elbow, look up, then straighten up and return to center. Bend forward slightly and repeat on the other side. Finish this series by rising on the toes again with the elbows flexing back, then lower the heels.

With the hands still clasped behind your head, bring the elbows together in front of the face. Bend at the knees, keeping your back straight, and slowly squat all the way down with the feet flat and knees apart. Now, curl forward and try to touch your toes or the insides of your ankles with your elbows. (Don't worry, you'll be able to curl forward more with practice!)

Straighten the legs, then slowly straighten the back, uncurling the back one vertebrae at a time, then the neck and head. (As an alternative, you may uncurl first so your back is straight, then stand up very slowly to avoid getting dizzy.) Come up slowly from the crouched position, and be careful in case of hypertension. When you are standing straight, rise on the toes again with the elbows flexing back, then lower the heels and bring the clasped hands over the head and down in front of the forehead.

Push your hands up above your head, fingers still interlaced and palms up, extending the arms, and rise up on your toes. Again be sure that you are keeping your entire back straight. Bring your hands back down in front of the forehead, palms down, while lowering the heels.

Bend sideways at the waist to the left as you bring the hands again to the top of your head, then repeat the arm extension with fingers still interlaced and palms up. At the same time, rise slightly on your toes if you are comfortable doing so (see Figure 2). Lower the heels, and lower the hands back in front of the forehead, palms down, and stand straight. Repeat on the other side.

Conclude by rising on your toes and extending your arms directly above your head, palms up. Now separate the hands, and lower them down the front of the body to the lower abdomen. Each time you push up and to the sides you can look toward the backs of the hands to help move your energy, if comfortable doing so, as long as you do not raise the head up. Instead, maintain the chin slightly tucked in (keeping the neck straight) as your eyes roll up and then follow your hands down.

BREATHING: Inhale when bringing the hands up and exhale when bending back. Inhale when straightening up and exhale when bending forward. Inhale when going up on the balls of the feet and when straightening back up. Exhale when twisting to look up and when bending over. Inhale when extending the hands above the head. Exhale when bringing the hands in front of the forehead and when lowering the hands at the end.

1.E Water and Fire Meet
Bend forward at the waist, placing palms on insides of ankles. Making small circles, slowly rub up the inside of the legs and down the outside, progressively moving the circles upward to the waist, drawing energy up the inside of the legs. When circling close to the waist, the circles resemble those in "The Dolphin's Fins Pat the Water," with the backs of the hands touching.

The last time you draw up to the waist with the backs of the hands together, bring the hands higher up the midline, fingers pointing downward, as you rise slightly on your toes and arch backward, until your hands are resting by your collarbones. You can think of this as raising the water energy from the ankle area to above the heart.

Lower heels and bend forward slightly, allowing your elbows to fall downward and your hands to come back down to the heart center.

With fingers pointing in toward the center of the chest, circle the elbows up in front, out and to the back, and down again. Leave the hands loose so the fingers will circle around the chest, moving up the midline, out the sides, down, and back in to the center. Allow the hands to move enough to let the elbows swing in large circles. Raise the

Figure 15

heels slightly when your elbows move up (see Figure 15). Then reverse the direction of the circles to go back to front. Do the same number in each direction.

Then circle one elbow at a time, twisting the upper body and moving the elbow on the left from front to back, then bringing the elbow back down and in, and repeating on the other side, alternating sides somewhat like doing the backstroke in swimming. Repeat several times. Then reverse the directions of the circles, moving the elbows back to front on the right side and then the left. Do the same number in each direction. You can think of all these circles as guiding the water energy to circulate in the "heart fire" area.

With the fingers over the center of the chest, bend forward slightly with the elbows in front, then pull the hands up the midline, lifting the elbows up and back and arch backward slightly. Straighten back up and bring the hands near the center of chest, then raise the heels and push the arms apart, moving them straight out to the sides, palms facing out (see Figure 45). When the arms are fully extended, flex the hands so the fingers point up; you should feel a gentle pull or tug on the middle finger. Relax the arms, slightly pulling the hands back, then push out again, and repeat several times. (Alternatively, the hands may be pulled back to the center of the chest and pushed out from there for several repetitions before closing.) Relax the hands, lower the heels and return the hands near the heart center, then close by lowering the hands to the lower *tan tien*.

BREATHING: Inhale when circling the hands up the insides of the legs, when pulling the hands up the midline, during the upward expansive half of each elbow circle, and when bringing the hands to the heart center before and after pushing the hands to the sides. Exhale when circling the hands down the outside of the legs, when lowering the hands back down to the heart center, during the downward contracting half of each elbow circle, when pushing the hands to the sides, and when lowering the hands at the end.

2. SECOND TREASURE:
Drawing the Bow with Both Hands to Aim at a Distant Target

Practicing the Second Treasure:
• Slowly gain flexibility through consistent practice rather than by forcing.

• Make your movements smooth so that the energy circulates.
• Make the movements gentle and flowing from your internal energy rather than from muscular force.
• Some movements may require some practice before you can allow the movements to flow gracefully.

2.A The Great Bird Spreads Its Wings

Start with feet wide apart (width of horse stance, but with legs straight). Bend forward at the waist, legs straight (but not locked), head down and hands hanging down almost touching the ground. Cross the arms at the wrists, right over left, with the palms facing up. Slowly and gently rock up and down with your back. Keep your upper body and arms relaxed, and let your arms swing freely at the shoulders. You will find that they tend to swing back and forth. Don't force them, simply allow the momentum to carry the arms. The arms should be totally relaxed and swing freely with no stiffness. The mild bouncing stimulates your spine. Do this until you have completely exhaled, benefiting the lungs and respiratory system.

Figure 16

Pause when your back and arms are down, then slowly bend at the knees and straighten up, while keeping the back at the same angle relative to the thighs and the hands in front of the chest. This will rotate you into the "horse stance" (as if you were astride a horse), with the arms extended horizontally and the palms facing inward toward the heart center. Make sure your hips are tucked slightly forward so that your spine including the lower back is straight.

Remaining in the horse stance, draw the hands in toward the heart center. Then push the hands straight out to the sides, palms facing out (see Figure 16). As the arms are fully extended to the sides, the fingers should be pointing straight up (exactly the same as in the end of the previous movement, Water and Fire Meet). Draw the hands back in to meet in front of the heart center, then lower them to close at the lower *tan tien*.

BREATHING: Inhale before bending over and rocking, when coming back up into the horse stance, and when drawing the hands back together near the end. Completely exhale when rocking up and down, pushing the hands apart, and lowering them at the end.

2.B Drawing the Bow

Start with feet wide apart (horse stance width). Bend the right knee and twist at the waist to turn your upper body facing right. As you do so, extend your left arm out to sweep with the momentum from left to right, finishing with the left hand in front of the right shoulder. Straighten the right leg. Bend the left knee and repeat the turning and sweeping motion with the right arm, so both arms are crossed in front of the chest, left under right.

Figure 17

Bend both knees to sit into a horse stance, and draw an imaginary bow string to the right with your right hand as you extend the left arm straight out to the left side, holding an imaginary bow (see Figure 17). As you do so, the eyes follow the index finger. Focus your eyes on your left index finger, which is pointing straight up; then look past the finger and refocus into the distance (at the "target"). This is also a good eye exercise.

Be sure your shoulders are relaxed; your chest should feel open. Feel the stretch across the chest. Your right elbow will be extended to the right side, not pointing behind. Also, feel the pull on the top of the index finger as it points straight up, stimulating the Large Intestine channel. Keep your back straight, not leaning in any direction. Then straighten the legs, lower the hands and face forward. Reverse to do the movement on the other side. (Alternatively, the arms can be kept up, sweeping the hands horizontally through the leg and waist motion to transition from one side to the other without lowering the arms in between repetitions.)

Repeat this entire movement several times.

BREATHING: Inhale when sweeping the arms around on each side to bring the hands into position. Exhale when drawing the bow, and lowering the arms.

2.C The Unicorn Turns Its Head to Look at the Moon

Start with heels together, or with feet slightly less than shoulder width apart, if necessary. Beginning with your hands at the sides, raise the hands out on both sides and above the head, then draw them down in front of the body.

When the hands reach the middle *tan tien*, pivot on the heel of the left foot and the ball of the right foot, turning left 180 degrees to face the opposite direction as you continue to circle the arms downward. With your legs crossed, place your weight on the left foot, which will be in front. Raise the arms to the sides and up again, then as you draw them down to be crossed in front of the

Figure 18

middle *tan tien*, left inside right, bend the knees and sit down on the legs. Only bend the knees as low as you feel comfortable, while keeping your lower back straight and relaxed. Also see Figure 1.

Twist the upper body to the left as your right hand draws the bow string, while the left hand extends with the left index finger pointing straight up, holding the bow. Your left arm extends out to your left side and up, not behind your back. However, because your upper body is twisted to the left, you should be pointing close to the original direction you were facing at the beginning of this movement. This twists and stretches your torso.

As you draw the bow, follow with your eyes the index finger of the extended hand (see Figure 1 and 18), which is stretched pointing up toward the "moon." At night, look up at the moon. During daytime, aim at an imaginary moon.

Staying low, un-twist the upper body and make a gathering movement with the arms at chest level, pulling the arms in front of the chest with wrists crossed again, and repeat the bow-drawing movement. Repeat several times.

Untwist to the right and straighten up slowly. Reverse the feet's pivot (left heel and ball of right foot) to face in the original direction, circling the left and then the right arm so they come in front of the chest with wrists crossed again. Lower arms and hands to the lower abdomen.

Reverse direction and repeat on the other side.

HINT: Beginners may bend the knees slightly instead of squatting low. Be sure to pivot and twist toward the same direction, like turning smoothly in a circle. If you are able to, perform this movement with heels together. Otherwise, use the open form with feet slightly apart.

BREATHING: Inhale when circling the arms upward, sweeping the arms inward into position to draw the bow, and untwisting at the end. Exhale when circling the arms downward, when drawing the bow, and lowering the hands at the end.

2.D Drawing the Precious Sword from Its Sheath

Start with feet wide apart (horse stance width). Gather energy by extending your left arm out to the left side, then bend the right knee and circle your left hand down and then up toward your chest. While you are circling the left arm in this way, the right arm swings out at chest level to the right side. Then bend the left knee

and reverse this gathering motion. Repeat this several times on both sides. Also be sure to shift the weight and turn the waist as you gather energy through these arm movements.

Step into a left cat stance as the left arm circles down and up by the waist, this time leaving the right arm in front of the chest, right hand by the left shoulder with the palm facing down. The left hand should be slightly below the right elbow with the palm facing up. In the cat stance, your weight should be on the right foot with your right knee bent. Bend the left knee with only the toes of the left foot lightly touching the ground.

Figure 19

Step out to the left side into a left bow stance, "uncoiling" by rotating your waist to face left. As you "uncoil," your left hand will "draw the sword" from the right side of your waist by moving slightly up with your left forearm in front of your chest, palm facing down. At the same time, push your right hand straight down by the front of your right leg, pushing palm down (as if holding the sword's sheath in place). See Figure 19 and 75. Pause, but continue the exhale (do not hold your breath).

Face front again, and repeat on the other side.

Repeat this entire movement, alternating sides, several times. After the first time on each side, you may omit the gathers before each "drawing of the sword." Then bring the hands together in front of the heart center and lower them to close.

HINTS: The movement originates from the waist. Keep the hand that "draws the sword" at about chest level and the other hand that "holds the sheath" pushing down, arm fully extended. This is a dispersing movement.

Optionally, you can add another series that is the same except that instead of "drawing the sword" from the waist or hip, you draw the hands to be in front of the chest, palms down and elbows bent, as if you are opening up the heart center. This movement resembles drawing the sword from a sheath at the shoulder or separating tall grass.

BREATHING: Inhale at the beginning when gathering to the chest with the arm on the same side you will step to, drawing back into the cat stance for each side, and bringing the hands together in front of the heart center at the end. Exhale when gathering to the chest with the opposite arm, when "uncoiling" to draw the sword, and when lowering the hands to close.

2.E Moving the Mountain and Pouring Out the Sea

Start with feet shoulder-width apart. Bring the hands up on the right side, then begin to trace a large circle in front of you with your hands, from the right side, above the head to the left, down the left side, across in front of the knees to the right, and back up on the right side. Turn the waist in the direction of the hands, and bend and straighten the legs to follow the hands down and up, assisting the circling motion. Repeat this gathering motion several times in the same direction.

After a few times around, as the arms swing past the knees, shift your weight to the right leg. Your knees will be bent, as you are in the left "cat stance" (described previously). Step out to the left side with the left foot and shift your weight onto the left foot with the left knee bent and the right leg straight. As you do so, bring your hands above the shoulders with the fingers pointing in toward the neck on each side. Then move your hands up until they are past the level of the top of your head, palms facing up (see Figure 20), and look up toward the hands without bending the neck back, to help move your energy.

Your body should form a straight line from the right leg, along the torso, up to the head. Next, bend the right knee and shift your weight back onto your right foot, circling the hands down and in to the heart center. Again, push the hands up over

Figure 20

the head as your weight moves left and straighten the right leg. Repeat this gathering and pushing motion several times.

Gently lower the hands to the lower tan tien as you return to a standing position. Repeat the entire movement on the other side.

HINT: The strength of the movement comes from shifting the weight with your legs and pushing at the same time. This movement pushes the energy from the chest past the ear area. Your hands guide the energy up the sides of your body to the top of your head.

Keep a side plane; that is, the elbow that's down should be pointing to the ground, and the elbow that's up should be pointing to the sky. Most people have a tendency to rotate so that the upper elbow points in front of them instead of straight up.

BREATHING: Inhale at the beginning when circling up with the arms, when drawing back before pushing out, and as you initially lower the hands just before the close. Exhale when circling down with the arms, pushing out, and finishing the close to the lower *tan tien*.

3. THIRD TREASURE:
Raising the Hands to Adjust the Stomach And Spleen

Practicing the Third Treasure:
• Remember to keep using your waist turns to move the arms and give momentum to the movements.
• Continue to ensure that your spine remains straight.

3.A The Jade Plate Receives the Morning Dew
Start with the heels together (or optionally, have feet apart to help you balance). Make a beak with your right hand and place it at the base of the spine, pointing up. Twist the waist right to place your left hand, palm up, by your right hip. Bend the knees; uncoil the waist to make a smooth sweeping motion with your left arm from your right hip to low on the left side. Straighten the knees; continue turning the waist to the left, sweeping the arm around to the left side, behind the body and up, and then bring the hand (with the palm still facing up) behind the head at about the level of the crown. Keeping the hands in position, bend forward slightly at the waist.

Figure 21

Next, rise up on the balls of your feet, simultaneously pushing the left hand (palm up) above the head and pushing the right hand (palm down) straight down (see Figure 21). Then, lower the heels, bend forward slightly, and retract both hands (the right hand in a beak at the lower back and the left hand near the crown). Repeat several times.

Return the right hand in a beak to the base of the spine and sweep the left hand, palm up, back down and around by the right hip, at the level of the middle *tan tien*. Release the right hand and sweep both arms to the left, at the level of the middle *tan tien*. Place the left hand in a beak at the base of the spine, and repeat the movement on the other side. When done, bring the hands together in front of the middle *tan tien*, then lower them.

HINTS: Move the palm as carefully as if you had a cup of water in it. Keep the palm up so as not to "spill the morning dew from the jade plate." The palms are always up, except when the beaked hand in back is pushing palm down. When the arm sweeps across the front, bend the knees as low as you can; otherwise, the knees are not bent. Keep the head and neck straight, but follow the sweeping motion of the hand with your eyes. The eyes follow the hand around the front to the back of the body. During the stretch, look up toward the hand, but without bending the neck back.

BREATHING: Inhale when sweeping one hand around in front and when bending forward slightly with the hand by the crown before pushing up, and when bringing the hands together in front of the middle *tan tien* at the end. Exhale when sweeping both hands around in front, when pushing the hands apart, and when lowering the hands at the end.

3.B Looking at the Lotus Flower in the Clear Pond

Start with heels together. Bring the hands up on the right side, then trace the beginning of a large circle in front of you with your hands, from the right side, down across in front of the knees, up on the left side, and up over the head to the right. Turn the waist in the direction of the hands, and bend and straighten the legs to follow the hands down and up, assisting the circling motion. After the arms swing up to the left, keep the forearms and hands facing upward, bend forward slightly, and bring the hands into position with the left palm facing the left ear slightly behind the head and the right palm facing left, slightly to the right of the heart center in front of the body.

Twist your upper body to the left so your right shoulder comes under your chin, pushing to the left with the right palm under the left arm with fingers pointing up, and pushing to the right

Figure 22

with the left palm behind the neck with fingers pointing down. Both wrists are flexed. Look down behind the right shoulder to gaze at your right foot (see Figures 22 and 44). During this movement, the left side should be stretched and the right upper chest compressed.

Untwist and relax, returning to face forward with the right hand in front and the left hand by the left ear. Repeat several times.

Drop the hands on the left side, and repeat the movement on the other side. When done, bring the hands together in front of the heart center and lower them to close.

HINT: Instead of turning the head or neck to gaze at the foot, be sure to twist the upper torso in order to bring your shoulder under your chin. Don't bend over trying to look down; keep the body upright, and look down.

BREATHING: Inhale at the beginning when circling up with the arms, when bending forward slightly each time before twisting and pushing with the palms, and when bringing the hands to the heart center just before closing. Exhale when circling down in the gathers, when twisting and pushing with the palms, and when lowering the hands to close.

4. FOURTH TREASURE:
Turning The Head to Tonify the Nervous System

Practicing the Fourth Treasure:
• As with the other movements, stretch well but never strain.
• Rotate very slowly and carefully.

4.A Turning the Head to Look at Your Star
Start with heels together and hands together in front of the heart center, palms down. Men place right hand underneath left hand, women place left hand underneath right hand. Place the thumb of the upper hand inside thumb of lower hand, and the first joint of one of the fingers of the upper hand over the side of the big knuckle of the little finger on the lower hand.

Push the hands with palms down from the heart center on the right side, turning the waist and bending the legs, then circle the hands back in toward the lower *tan tien*. At the bottom of the circle, turn the palms over to face up and circle the hands with palms up back up on the left side. At the top, turn the palms over to face down, and continue circling several more times. Let the body sway with the circular motion.

After a few circles, press the hands with palms down to waist level on the right side until the arms are almost straight, and the hands are at the right side of the waist. Bend forward only very slightly, and turn the head toward the left side, turning the eyes to look up and behind you toward your "star" (see Figure 23). Pause as you continue exhaling. Straighten up and reverse the circling direction to bring the hands back up on the right side to the heart center.

Repeat this entire movement on the other side.

HINT: As you look at your star, keep your shoulders relaxed and feel the stretch at the side of the neck. Turn your eyes to the outside corner to exercise and stimulate them.

BREATHING: Inhale when hands move up, and exhale when they move down.

Figure 23

4.B Turning the Head to Contemplate Earth

Move your hands behind against the small of the back and place them in the same position as in the previous movement, except with the backs of the hands against the back and palms facing away. Rubbing the backs of the hands against the lower back, circle the hands down on the right, around behind the lower tan tien, up on the other side and returning to the small of the back. Continue circling around in the same direction a few more times. As you circle the hands, turn the waist and let your body sway with the circular motion.

After a few circles, press the hands with palms down to below waist level on the right side until the arms are almost straight. Turn the neck to look behind the left shoulder, to the highest point of the left ankle bone (see Figure 24). Pause as you continue exhaling.

Figure 24

Straighten up and reverse the circling direction to bring the hands back up on the right side to the small of the back. Relax and straighten.

Repeat this entire movement on the other side.

HINT: As you look down, keep your shoulders relaxed and feel the stretch at the side of the neck. Looking down stimulates the eyes and stretches the neck.

BREATHING: Inhale when hands move up, and exhale when they move down.

4.C The Weeping Willow Shivers in the Early Morning Breeze

Externally, this movement is the same as part of the Warm-Up. However, even though you have done it in the Warm-Up, do not skip it here because your energy is different now and you are circulating your *chi*.

Use the image of a willow tree in the wind. As it moves, it starts from the top and slowly moves down the "trunk." Be flexible like the willow tree.

1. Turning the neck

Start with heels together and hands together. Men place right hand underneath left hand, women place left hand underneath right hand. Place the thumb of the upper hand inside the thumb of the lower hand, and the first joint of one of the fingers of the upper hand over the side of the big knuckle of the little finger on the lower hand. Place the hands over the lower *tan tien*.

Keeping the neck relaxed, use the upper body and shoulders to roll the head gently and slowly to the left side, back, to the right, and front in a circle, repeating several times. See Figure 50.

Reverse direction with the head bent forward and repeat.

HINT: Eyes are almost closed, remaining slightly open to keep a subtle level of awareness. Rotate gently! Be sure that the head simply follows gravity as your upper body tilts slightly in all directions. Do not use your neck muscles at all. As you rotate, keep the hands at the lower *tan tien*.

BREATHING: Inhale as the head circles upward, exhale as it circles downward.

2. Turning the hips
Start with heels together, or farther apart if necessary for balance. Place the palms of the hands over the kidneys and rub them a few times to warm them up.

Keeping the palms over the kidneys, and the head upright and over the feet, push the hips forward, then to the left, back, to the right, and forward to make a complete rotation. Repeat several times.

While the hips are forward, reverse direction and repeat several more times in the opposite direction, then straighten up.

BREATHING: Exhale as the hips circle forward, inhale back.

3. Turning the knees
Start with feet together. Bend forward at the waist and rest the hands on the knees. Since you should be warmed up by now, it should not be necessary to rub the knees. Make a circle by bending the knees to the left (see Figure 25), then in front and to the right, and then straighten. Repeat several times.

Reverse the direction of the circles and repeat several times.

Next, make circles by bending the knees forward and separating them, moving them out to each side, and circling back as you straighten them. Repeat several times.

Reverse the direction of the circles and repeat several times.

BREATHING: Exhale when circling down, inhale when circling up.

Figure 25

Congratulations!

You have learned the first four of the Eight Treasures. If you have access to an instructor, this is a good time to review with him or her all the movements you have learned so far and clarify any questions about the correct postures, breathing, and any other aspect of the practices.

5. FIFTH TREASURE:
Swaying the Spinal Column to Take Away Heart Fire

Practicing the Fifth Treasure:
• All movements should flow continuously as part of an integral whole. Be sure to stay relaxed. Breathing smoothly, evenly and without hesitation is the key to a smooth flow of energy.
• All movements in this Treasure use the horse stance, as previously described. Sit as low as possible, but do not strain. Toes are ideally pointing straight ahead, but if there is pain or a strain on the knees, be sure to allow the toes to point out.
• Only do as much as is comfortable. Strength is built up through consistent practice.

5.A The Sleeping Lion Shifts Its Head and Awakens
Start with feet horse stance width apart and sit down into a horse stance. Keep the back straight and chin tucked in. Rest the wrists on the knees with palms down. The hands should be comfortably in front of the knees.

Slowly bend the torso from the waist sideways toward the left knee. Touch the left ear to the back of the left wrist (or get as close as possible). Look up to the right and pause (see Figures 26 and 73) as you continue the exhale. Reverse the movement and slowly return to an upright sitting position in the horse stance. Repeat on the right side.

Next, turn your hands palms up with the tips of the thumb and middle finger on each hand touching, resting your wrists on your knees. Rest the palm of the right hand on top of the right leg, and place the (outside) edge of the left hand at the base of the skull behind the left ear. (As an alternative, the right hand may be placed in the beak position at the base of the spine.) Keeping the hand behind the ear, slowly bend the torso from the waist sideways toward the left knee, twisting to bring the back of the left upper arm against the inside of the left knee. Twist the head to the right to look up over the right shoulder. Reverse the movement and slowly return to an upright sitting position in the horse stance. Reverse the hand positions, and repeat on the other side.

Figure 26

Place both hands palms up with the tips of the thumb and middle finger on each hand touching, resting your wrists on your knees, then slowly straighten up to a standing position, lowering the hands.

HINT: The whole torso is turned slightly in the first part, and a little more during the second part. Turn the torso more to reduce neck strain. Remember, we are not doing anything to the head, so keep it aligned with the spine so as not to strain the neck.

Keep the lower back straight and the tailbone curled or tucked in. Look up to the side as far as you can to stretch your neck. End both parts with arms forward, hands resting on the knees with index fingers curled up touching the thumbs.

BREATHING: Inhale when sitting into the horse stance in the beginning, and when straightening up after bending to the side each time. Exhale when bending to the side, and when lowering the hands at the end.

5.B Lying Down to Watch the Constellations

Start with the feet horse stance width apart. Make a beak with the right hand, at the base of the spine. Bring the left hand over your left shoulder, behind your head, and around to the right side. Keeping left elbow pointing up behind your head, curl your fingers around the right side of the jaw or chin, or the right ear. Sit into the horse stance, then slowly bend the torso from the waist sideways toward the left knee, then turn and twist the upper body to the right, looking up on the right side. Look up and pause (see Figure

Figure 27

27) as you continue exhaling. Reverse the movement, and slowly return to an upright standing position, lowering the hands. Repeat on the other side.

HINT: The torso is turned as much as possible in this movement, more than in the previous movements.

Keep the lower back straight and the tailbone curled or tucked in. Look up to the side as far as you can to stretch your neck.

BREATHING: Inhale when bringing the hand up to the head, and when straightening up after bending down each time. Exhale when bending down and when lowering the hands at the end of the movement.

6. SIXTH TREASURE:
Raising the Heels to Remove Physical and Mental Weakness

Practicing the Sixth Treasure:
• These movements seem simpler, especially after the Fifth Treasure. Be sure to keep the mind focused on each movement to help you stay alert.
• The jarring movements of this Treasure stimulate the spine; do them moderately.

6.A Bringing the Stream Back to the Sea
Start with heels together and hands together. Men place right hand underneath left hand, women place left hand underneath right hand. Place the thumb of the upper hand inside the thumb of the lower hand, and the first joint of one of the fingers of the upper hand over the side of the big knuckle of the little finger on the lower hand. Place the hands over the lower *tan tien*.

Raise the heels and inhale with the focus on the lower *tan tien* (see Figure 28). Drop the heels and exhale. Repeat several times.

HINT: Dropping down to shake the spine causes a slight vibrational stimulation all the way up the body. Keep the chin slightly tucked so the vibration can go all the way up the spine to the head, into the base of the skull and brain. Avoid high impact to prevent mild concussion; you just need a small amount for a *chi* flow.

Keep the spine straight, do not tense the lower back. Do the movement slowly and meditatively.

BREATHING: Inhale as you rise on the balls of the feet. Exhale after the impact.

Figure 28

6.B Pumping the Water from the Origin of the Fountain

Start with the feet horse stance width apart. Bending forward at the waist, grasp the ankles from behind with the hands. Lift the heels, using the upper body (torso and arms) to pull up at the ankles, pulling upward as you inhale (see Figure 29). Drop the heels, exhale and relax. Repeat this several times, then slowly straighten up.

HINT: Grab and lift the heels up as high as you can. Be sure to lift! You should feel that you are pulling up or lifting with the inhale and pulling your ankles, not pushing up with the feet. Then when you go down, don't push down but simply drop for a slight impact. Keep the legs straight (although never locked).

Figure 29

BREATHING: Inhale as you rise on the balls of the feet. Exhale after the impact.

7. SEVENTH TREASURE:
Tightening the Tendons to Reinforce Yourself

Practicing the Seventh Treasure:
• All movements in this Treasure are done with the feet horse stance width apart.
• Make rapid movements well-coordinated and smooth, and stay relaxed.
• "Tighten the tendons" at the moment when a movement calls for extension of the arms; otherwise, keep the arms relaxed.
• Pause after each rapid movement for the energy follow-through.

7.A Pushing Down the Fierce Tiger
Start with feet horse stance width apart. Bend forward at the waist, and reach down toward the feet, placing palms on the inside of ankles. Straighten up slowly, drawing the hands up the insides of the legs, across the abdomen and part way up the chest, bringing them in front of the heart center with the palms down. Start to slowly sink the knees and hands, then relax and drop, bending the knees and pushing the palms straight down between your knees (see Figure 30). At the bottom of the drop, flex the wrists so the palms are parallel to the ground.

Repeat several times. Return to an upright position.

HINT: When you feel comfortable with the movement, raise the heels slightly each time you drop.

BREATHING: Inhale when drawing the hands up, exhale when lowering them and dropping.

Figure 30

7.B The Tiger Grabs Its Prey

Start with feet horse stance width apart. Circle the arms up and out in front to meet at the level of the face with wrists crossed and palms facing inward, then draw them back down and in to the lower *tan tien*. After the arms drop fully, extend them to circle out again. Repeat several times.

Next, bend the knees as the arms descend. Quickly rise by pushing up with the legs, straightening the knees, straightening the back, and allowing the momentum to carry the arms straight out in front, projecting the hands up and out from the lower *tan tien* (see Figure 31). As this wave of energy reaches the hands, tighten the hands so the thumbs and all fingers point down as "tiger claws" (this is very similar to the beak shape). Repeat several times.

Figure 31

Next, change the direction of the upward movement "grabbing the prey" to the left, turning toward the left as you rise into a left bow stance (See Figure 49). Repeat several times to the left, repeat once to the center, then repeat on the right side with an equal number of motions.

Finish by doing one motion to the front, then gently lower hands.

HINT: Keep the upper body and shoulders relaxed. Do not push the shoulders forward, or lean forward; keep your posture upright.

BREATHING: Inhale when drawing the hands down and in toward the lower tan tien. Exhale when moving the hands up and out, and when projecting the hands to "grab the prey."

7.C Clench the Teeth, Widen the Eyes and Strike to the Four Directions

Start with the feet horse stance width apart. Gather energy by extending your arms out to the left, and then drawing the left hand in toward your chest. As you bring the left hand in, the right arm

swings out to the right. As previously explained, you create the momentum for this by bending the knee and shifting the weight in the direction of the arm swing. Re-
peat the gather on the other side. Do this several times. On the last swing to the left, bend both knees, turn the waist to the left, and bring both hands by the left hip. The right hand's palm is down with fingers extended, and the left hand is in a fist, fingers up.

Figure 32

First you will do a single punch. Untwist the waist and punch forward with the left fist straight out in front, palm down. As you do this, keep shoulders square and bring the right arm to the side so your right hand (in a fist with palm up) is by the right hip (see Figure 32). For this punch, and all that follow, clench the teeth and widen the eyes, looking in the direction of the punch, when striking. Repeat the gather and punch on the other side.

HINT: The force of the punch comes from the waist (*tan tien*), not the arms. Do not lock the elbow. Keep the shoulders relaxed, and do not extend the striking arm's shoulder forward or lean forward.

When making a fist, keep the thumb outside the fist. Tighten the fist only at the punch.

Next you will do double punches. After a gathering motion, repeat the left-hand single punch. After the punch, bend both knees and punch with the right hand as the left fist pulls back to the left hip. Rise and punch left, drop and punch right. Repeat several times. Then, initiate the gathering motion on the right side and repeat the double punches starting with the right fist.

HINT: Whenever you punch with one hand, bring the other hand down by the hip.

Next you will punch to each side. After the gathering motion, turn hips and waist to face right as you rise into a right bow stance, and do a single left-hand punch toward the right. Repeat on the other side.

Finish by repeating the single punches to the front, punching with the left fist, then with the right fist. Bring the hands together in front of the middle *tan tien*, then lower them to close.

BREATHING: Inhale when gathering in with the hand that will punch next, and extend the inhale just before striking when you circle the hands to the side of the waist. Also inhale when bringing the hands back together in front of the middle *tan tien* at the end. Exhale for the opposite direction of the gathers, punching, and lowering the hands at the end.

7.D The Tiger Gathers Its Energy and Crouches

Start with feet horse stance width apart. Circle the arms up and out to the front to meet at the level of the face with wrists crossed and palms facing inward, then draw them back to the level of the lower *tan tien*. After the arms drop fully, extend them to circle out again. Repeat several times.

After a few circles, when the hands are above the head, make loose fists and drop in one quick motion by bending the knees and drawing the arms in to cross wrists at the level of the lower *tan tien* (see Figure 33). Circle the arms back up and out, and repeat several times.

HINT: Do not touch the body when dropping and gathering the *chi* into the lower *tan tien*. When making a fist, keep the thumb outside the fist. Tighten the fist at the bottom of the drop.

Figure 33

BREATHING: Inhale when drawing the hands down and in toward the lower *tan tien*, both during the initial gathers and when dropping into the crouch. Exhale when circling the hands up and out.

8. EIGHTH TREASURE:
Grabbing the Ankles to Strengthen Your Vital Force

Practicing the Eighth Treasure:
• The first four movements of this Treasure are done in the horse stance.
• When doing the balancing movements, the center of gravity is the lower *tan tien* (lower abdomen); concentrate on the weighted foot.
• It helps in keeping your balance if you focus your vision on one small, stationary object in front of you, and bend the weighted knee.
• When bending your back and trunk, move slowly and do not strain.

8.A The White Crane Washes Its Wing Feathers
Start in the horse stance. Extend your arms out and up on both sides, bringing them up above the head. Clasp hands together behind the head with fingers interlaced and bend forward at the waist, bringing elbows near knees.

Figure 34

Turn the left side up, bracing the right elbow against the inside of the right knee, and pulling the left elbow up and back. Twist the upper body and left elbow back, looking up (see Figure 34). Return to the center, then repeat on the other side. Repeat this movement several times, alternating sides.

Finish by returning to center, then rise to a standing position, then unclasp and lower hands.

HINT: The thumbs should be placed at the base of the skull. You should feel a pleasant stretch of the lower back over the kidney.

BREATHING: Inhale when twisting to look up and when straightening back up. Exhale when bending over, changing from one side to the other, and lowering the hands at the end.

8.B The White Crane Turns Its Head to Look Up

Start in the horse stance. Bend forward at the waist, resting hands on knees with the fingers of opposite hands pointing toward each other. The bend makes an "L" shape, so your upper body is horizontal to the ground and at a 90-degree angle from the legs.

Keeping the neck straight, slowly rotate the head as far as you can toward the left to look up (see Figure 35), then turn the head back to the center. Repeat on the other side.

Repeat several times. Finish by returning the head to center, looking straight down, then stand up slowly.

HINT: Keep the chin slightly tucked, so you use the neck to turn the head. Look out of the corner of the eye when you look up; this exercises and stimulates the eye.

BREATHING: Inhale when turning the head to the side to look up and

Figure 35

when straightening back up at the end. Exhale when bending over, when returning the head to center, and when lowering the hands at the end.

8.C The White Crane Twists Its Body to Look Up

Start in the horse stance. Bend forward at the waist. Rest your left

Figure 36

hand on the left knee (thumb can be just inside the knee), and reach to the left with the right hand to grasp the inside of the left ankle. Bend the right knee, and shift your weight onto your right foot, straightening the left leg. At the same time, twist the body left and turn your head left to look up. Push gently with the hand on the knee and pull gently with the hand on the ankle to help the twist (see Figure 36). Unwind, shift the weight back and slowly straighten up to standing position. Repeat on the other side.

Repeat the entire movement several times.

HINT: Keep both heels on the ground throughout the movement.

Keep the rear as low as possible. While inhaling, twist the body around and look up as far as you can without slouching over and losing the natural uprightness in your trunk.

BREATHING: Inhale when twisting the body to the side to look up and when straightening back up at the end. Exhale when reaching to grasp the legs, when changing sides, and closing.

8.D The White Crane Sharpens Its Beak

Start in the horse stance. Circle arms out and up on the sides, and clasp hands behind the head, fingers interlaced, thumbs placed at the base of the skull. Turn the waist to the left, and bend forward at the waist until your nose is as close to the left knee as is comfortably possible (keeping both legs straight). Slide clasped hands down

Figure 37

over the head and then back up in front of the face, then down the leg to the outer left ankle (see Figure 37). Pause, then slowly straighten up and face forward, releasing the hands and lowering them.

Repeat the entire movement on the other side.

HINT: As an option, if it feels more comfortable, you can turn the foot out in the direction you are bending. Also, after pushing down along the leg, you may grasp the ankle with both hands and gently pull the head and trunk of the body in against the leg for more of a stretch.

BREATHING: Inhale when bringing the hands up to clasp behind the head, when bringing them back up in front of the face, and when straightening up each time. Exhale when bending over, when pushing down along the leg and stretching, and when lowering the hands at the end.

8.E The White Crane Strengthens Its Vital Force

Start with feet together. Circle arms out and up on the sides, and clasp hands behind head, fingers interlaced, thumbs at base of skull. Slowly bend forward at the waist. Touch nose to knees (see Figure 38). Slide clasped hands down over the head, then back up in front of the face, then down the legs to the feet. Pause as you continue exhaling. Release hands and grasp ankles from the outside and back, and gently pull torso toward legs. Slowly straighten up, releasing the hands and lowering them.

Figure 38

NOTE: People with low back problems should be cautious about forcing the stretch of the lumbar. Perform the bending in a graduated fashion.

HINT: Legs remain straight, but as always, never lock the knees.

BREATHING: Inhale when bringing the hands up to clasp behind the head, when bringing them back up in front of the face, when reaching around to grasp the ankles, and when straightening up. Exhale when bending over, when pushing down the leg, when stretching, and when lowering the hands at the end.

8.F The White Crane Stretches Its Legs Behind and Forward

Start both sections with the feet together.

1. Behind:

Circle the arms down and out to the sides, then up over the head. Lower arms, crossing wrists in front of the body. Circle arms back up and out to sides, and raise your left knee. In a continuous motion, make beaks with both hands, bring the hands down on both sides of the chest, and extend both arms and the left leg straight out behind you. Leg, arms and head are all horizontal (forming a "T" shape); the beaks point up (see Figure 39). Pause, holding the

Figure 39

exhale. Circle the arms back up, bringing the arms and the leg to the front again as you straighten, with knee bent and hands over the head. Slowly lower leg and arms, crossed at the wrists, and return to a normal standing position.

Repeat on the other side.

HINT: Slightly bend the weighted knee for better balance. Use the lower abdomen as the center of gravity. Beginners may hold a chair on one side to practice the movement. Keeping the lower back straight or slightly tucked is beneficial and also may help balance.

BREATHING: Inhale when raising hands over head, and when straightening back up after extending the leg. Exhale when lowering the hands, and as you extend the leg backward; hold the breath when pausing. Exhale when lowering the hands at the close.

2. Forward:

Circle the arms down and out to the sides, then up over the head. Lower arms, crossing wrists in front of the body. Circle arms back up and out to the sides, then bring them in toward the heart center. At the same time, raise your left knee. Extend the hands straight forward, palms facing out, while you straighten the left knee so the leg is also extended horizontally straight forward. No beaks form when leg stretches forward; instead, flex hands back at the wrist.

Slowly bend the right knee as low as you can (with practice, all the way down until you are in a squatting position), with your left leg and arms extended straight forward (see photo on front cover). Pause, holding the exhale. Then straighten the right knee, rising up with the left leg and the arms extended. When straightened up, bend the left knee while bringing the hands in, and circle the hands up over the head. Slowly lower the left leg and hands, crossed at the wrists, returning to a standing position.

Repeat the entire movement on the other side.

HINT: Keep the weight of the upper body slightly forward when squatting and standing with the leg extended. Beginners may balance themselves by holding onto a chair; you may also try grabbing the extended leg or foot with both hands. The movement helps strengthen the legs, which is important for retaining vitality during your life and into old age.

To bend the knee all the way down, the ankle must be flexible and strong. Inhale into the *tan tien* and thrust yourself up with leg still straight forward. Inflate the "balloon" in your abdomen.

BREATHING: Inhale when raising hands over head, and when straightening back up after extending the leg. Exhale when lowering the hands, and as you extend the leg forward; hold the breath when pausing. Exhale when lowering the hands at the close.

Figure 40

8.G The White Crane Guards the Plum Flower Proudly Standing Alone on the Cold Mountain

Start with the feet together. Raise the left leg and grasp the ankle with both hands, pulling the left leg against the chest. Bend the right leg to lower the body, and tilt the upper body slightly forward, bending at the waist. Then straighten the right leg and the back, raising up while pulling the left leg close to the body (see Figure 40). Repeat several times. Slowly release and lower left leg.

Repeat for the other leg.

HINT: Beginners may grasp the leg below the knee with one hand, and the ankle with the opposite hand.

BREATHING: Inhale when you pull the leg upward, focusing on the kidney on that side. Exhale when sinking downward, and when lowering the leg and hands at the end.

8.H The White Crane Limbers Its Wings

1. First part

Start with heels together. Extend arms to the sides, palms facing forward. With arms straight and horizontal to the ground, bring palms together in front. Bend the elbows to bring the hands to the front of the chest, keeping palms together and fingers pointing forward. Extend hands in front again. Rotate the hands, thumbs down, bringing the backs of the hands together. Flex wrists so the hands bend back and the fingers curl toward the body, then relax the wrists and bend the elbows, circling the hands with backs together so that the fingers point down, then toward the chest, up, and back forward again. Keep the backs of hands together as much as possible until the fingers point forward again, and then turn the palms up as the arms extend forward.

Make fists and draw the hands back along the sides of the waist and behind the back. As the hands pull back along the kidneys in the waist area, pack the energy into the kidneys. Bringing the hands behind the back, clasp them together and lift the arms upward as you bend forward at the waist. As you lift the arms, rotate them backward and upward as much as possible, stretching the shoulder muscles.

Bring the arms back down as you bend the knees and squat, straightening the upper body as your clasped hands circle under the buttocks. Release the hands and extend them straight forward, palms facing down. Stand up slowly, with the arms extended in front of the chest.

Repeat the entire movement. Then lower the hands to close.

HINT: Stretch the arms and raise the hands up as high as you can in the back. Keep hands together as they circle under the buttocks. This stretches and opens up the wing bone. Also, instead of clasping the hands in back, you can grasp one wrist the first time, and the other wrist the second time.

BREATHING: Inhale on movements toward the body, when lowering the arms to the waist, after stretching the arms up over the back, and when bringing the arms up in front. Exhale on movements away from the body (to the front), when lifting the arms in back to stretch the shoulder muscles, and when lowering the hands and squatting, and when lowering the hands at the end.

Figure 41

2. Second part

Start with feet shoulder-width apart. Circle the left arm out and up, then bend its elbow, placing left hand behind the left shoulder from above. As you do this, circle the right arm inward behind the back, and bend its elbow to place the right hand behind the back from below. Link the two hands (see Figure 41), or if they do not reach, grasp a towel or belt to link the two hands.

Bend forward slightly and twist to the left, circling down to the left, circle toward the center, bending down in front, then circle up on the right side, and straighten up. Repeat several times. When done, gently release the hands and lower them.

Reverse hands and repeat in the opposite direction.

HINT: Linking the two hands, such as by interlocking the fingers, pulls the arms and stretches the shoulder blades. As you circle the upper body you will also feel a good stretch of the lower back over each kidney.

BREATHING: Inhale when bending the arms into position in the beginning, when circling up, and when straightening up at the end of each side. Exhale when circling down and when lowering the hands at the end.

8.I The Dragon Flies Throughout the Heavens

Start with feet shoulder-width apart. Bring the hands over the head, forming loose fists. Begin slowly by tracing a large circle with the hands (See Figures 42 and 74), twisting the waist and pulling down the left side and into the lower *tan tien*. Continue by circling the hands up on the right side, over the head, and back down to the lower *tan tien* on the left side. Repeat several times. Pull with loose

Figure 42

fists down into the lower *tan tien* as though pulling a rope down and in.

After a few circles, continue by pulling the hands down on the left side quickly with some downward momentum, bending the knees and pulling the loose fists toward the lower *tan tien*. As you do so, inhale and fill the abdomen (lower *tan tien*) with the energy. Release the arms and slowly complete the circle, circling hands up on the right side. Repeat several times.

Repeat the entire movement in the other direction several times.

When finished, return to a centered standing position, knees slightly bent, arms extended in front at chest level, elbows slightly bent, palms down, and close by bringing the palms down in front of the lower *tan tien*.

HINT: You gather *chi* by the circular movement, then pack *chi* into the lower *tan tien*.

BREATHING: Inhale as the arms and hands come down and in toward the lower *tan tien*. Exhale as the arms move up and away from the lower *tan tien*.

C. Standing Meditation and Return of *Chi*

Stand with feet shoulder-width apart, spine straight, knees slightly bent, arms extended in front at chest level, elbows slightly bent, palms facing the heart center. The shoulders and elbows are relaxed, and the fingers pointing to each other a few inches apart. Hold this position for a few breaths or minutes. Be sure your back is straight and pelvis tipped forward (tucked in).

After a while, lower the hands in front of the lower *tan tien*, and hold this position, as you did for the heart center (see Figure 43 on page 78). When finished, relax and drop the hands so the arms hang loosely at the sides. This standing meditation is important for draining the *chi* down through the body into the lower *tan tien*, collecting and storing it.

Commentary:

Guide the *chi* to trickle down from the higher places of the head and chest area to the lower *tan tien*. Continue to stand quietly as you trickle the *chi* so that it runs back down from your upper body into your lower *tan tien*. As the *chi* moves down and the area at arm's level empties of *chi*, slowly move the arms down to reflect the level of the abundance of *chi* and to continue to guide the *chi* closer to your lower *tan tien*. You gather the energy there for a while and put it into storage. When you finish, inhale and then exhale. This meditation may last 5 to 10 minutes or longer.

The standing meditation is essential; it is among the most important parts of the Eight Treasures. Do not skip the closing meditation, because it allows your *chi* to return to be stored in your *tan tien*.

D. Walking

After the Eight Treasures, including the standing meditation, it is good to walk about to adjust your energy for the activities of every-day life. Five minutes or more of walking is good. As you do so, young and middle-age women as well as young men should return the focus to the heart center (middle *tan tien*) to carry their energy somewhat higher. Take a break of at least five minutes if you plan to follow the Eight Treasures practice with *t'ai chi*.

E. Tips for Beginning Students

Once you have learned a few movements, and are able to relax and let the mind and body work together, learning becomes easier and quicker. The first movements a student learns usually take a little longer, but this is only because you are learning a new way of moving. For many students, this is their first experience with inter-nal movement. Most people take a while to get used to totally relaxing, and not using the mind so much in thinking about the movement. This gets better with time and practice. In learning these movements, make sure to breathe from the lower abdomen, relax the lower back and shoulders, and keep a calm and happy mind. Learn the spirit of the movements, and fill in the details later.

Standing Meditation and Return of Chi
(Figure 43)

Section 3
Intermediate Practice

At the intermediate level, the focus is on refining what you have already learned, achieving a deeper state of relaxation while doing the movements and generally learning about chi.

Looking at the Lotus Flower in the Clear Pond
(Figure 44)

Chapter 4

Improving Your Practice

For beginning students, the most challenging movements seem to be: (First Treasure) *Move the Stars and Turn the Big Dipper*; (Second Treasure) *The Unicorn Turns Its Head to Look at the Moon* and *Drawing the Precious Sword from Its Sheath*; (Fourth Treasure) *Turning the Head to Contemplate Earth*; (Fifth Treasure) *The Sleeping Lion Shifts Its Head and Awakens* and *Lying Down to Watch the Constellations*; (Sixth Treasure) *Pumping the Water from the Origin of the Fountain*; (Seventh Treasure) *Clench the Teeth, Widen the Eyes, and Strike in the Four Directions*; and (Eighth Treasure) *The White Crane Stretches its Legs Behind and Forward*. Here are some pointers given by some experienced teachers to make each of these, and some other movements, easier to learn and do.

First Treasure:
Move the Stars and Turn the Big Dipper - In the first part of the movement (*Move the Stars*), the arms and hands are making circles. The horizontal circles are like creating a whirlpool of energy, which then gets drawn down into the body through the top of the head with the vertical circles. Another image is that of sweeping away cobwebs gathered in the head overnight (for morning practice) and then to draw in the energy as if you could drink the subtle energies of the heavens in through your head and swallow them directly down into your abdomen.

For the next part, imagine bringing good energy into the chest or heart area. In this part, many people tense their shoulders and upper backs. Relax your shoulders and let the stress and tension fall away. Keep the arms and hands below the shoulders, at about the level of your heart, and let them follow the waist.

When bringing the energy up from the ankle, be sure to come up slowly to avoid dizziness. People are often wobbly whenever they rise up off their heels. To help with this, in the second part of the movement (*Turn the Big Dipper*), some teachers recommend keeping the lower back straight and the breathing low. Another idea is to focus on the initiating energy coming from the top of the head raising the body up from above rather than pushing up from the ankles below. Another is to keep the shoulder down and relaxed, with the elbow pointing down. Also, finding the internal connection from the feet and ankles up the body to the eyes and then extending out to the fingers serves to unite the body in this movement and naturally maintain balance.

81

The Great Elephant Raises Its Trunk - People always have to repeat the part after gathering in to the waist, in order to remember when to keep the knees straight, when to bend them and how to coordinate the gathering with the arms. In the first part, the arms are drawing the energy in while the legs are rolling the energy up to the abdomen. In the second part, notice how the knees and arms go in and out together, setting the dynamic rhythm for this transition to the squatting circles.

Water and Fire Meet - In this movement, pay attention to how the arms and elbows circle in connection with the rocking motion of the body. The key is to remember this is not just an arm movement, but a whole body movement. The arms are like the branches of a living tree, while the trunk is the source of the power connected to the roots. The rocking and swinging of the body is what creates the impetus for the arms and elbows to circle.

Second Treasure:

The Unicorn Turns Its Head to Look at the Moon - First learn how to turn around properly before adding the movement of the arms. Notice that we turn on the heel of one foot and the ball and toes of the other foot, bending the knees slightly and shifting the weight to maintain balance. When you turn left, use the left heel and shift the weight to the left; do the reverse when you turn right. Practice this a number of times until it feels comfortable. Then add the rest of the movement. The arm circles and the turn complement and give impetus for each other. There is a transfer of energy from the arms down through the legs bending into the turn. Then from the feet, it works its way back up, using the waist or lower *tan tien* as a pivot. You may keep the feet slightly apart, tucking the rear knee under the front knee after the turn for added stability. With the knees bent, follow the turning shoulder and draw the bow.

Drawing the Precious Sword from Its Sheath - You will want to practice the first part repeatedly to get the "rhythm" of the movement. Try it with one arm at a time, imagining the arms rising and sinking like ocean waves. This movement is common to many *t'ai chi* forms and is usually called "*Waving Hands Like Clouds.*" After the initial gathering, break down the movement this way: first, step to the side and slightly back so that you maintain a comfortable width between your feet when you turn, then turn the waist and hips, and finally draw the sword and express the energy through the hands. Your front foot and knee, your navel and nose should all face the same direction when you have completed the movement. Also at the end of the movement, bring the toes of the rear foot slightly in so the back leg participates in the *"One Chi"* of this movement. Generally, don't try to figure it out with your arms and upper body, just follow the shift of weight and direction and let the upper body follow the flow.

Fourth Treasure:

Turning the Head to Contemplate Earth - The movement comes again from the waist or lower *tan tien* and moves up and over from the placement of the hands, with the tip of your nose gently leading your head to look back over the shoulder and toward your ankle.

Fifth Treasure:

Don't overextend yourself in this treasure. Let the movements and flow of energy bring you to completion of the movements. Remember the name of this treasure (Swaying the Spinal Column to Take Away Heart Fire); really sway the spinal column as you go to each side with the movements. These swaying movements originate at the waist and the lower *tan tien* and easily unfold through the chest, arms, neck and head. If you have difficulty in the beginning, you can practice this section sitting on the edge of a chair or a stool. It will be easier for you to get a sense of how your waist and your *tan tien* initiate and control all of the swaying movements in this position. Remember to breathe with this movement! Students often hold their breath and then find themselves panting.

The Sleeping Lion Shifts Its Head and Awakens - It's good to start with small knee bends and a good wide stance and focus on deep "belly breathing": Inhale to begin, then exhale as you bring the ear toward the back of the wrist by the knee. You could "rest" in this posture for 2-3 deep breaths, but even if you cannot maintain this position that long, be sure to stay relaxed. Keeping the torso horizontal, turn the whole trunk and spine to look up rather than contorting the body parts one against the other. Then inhale again as you rise from the posture.

Lying Down to Watch the Constellations - The advice here is mostly the same as for the previous movement. Also, as you wrap your arm around your head, be sure not to strain your neck by pulling too hard on the head. Keep the elbow and the shoulder opened up. This way, you can keep the neck aligned with the spine, and also stimulate the Heart point in the armpit to gain the energy benefits of the movement.

About the Horse Stance, and the use of your legs and back

Many people have various misconceptions about how their legs bend. Ankles are often stiff and people often misuse their hip joints or knees. Don't forget to bend the ankles as you bend the legs. The bending of the legs occurs at all three major joints: the ankles, the knees and the hips. There is a direct connection between the knees and the toes: they should point in the same direction. Structurally the knee joint functions the same way as the elbow joint. Everyone understands experientially that the elbow bends only in one plane, and it would destroy the joint to attempt to bend the elbow laterally (lateral movement in the arms occurs at other joints). This is often much less clear with knee joints. Treat your knee joints like you treat your elbows. Bring your knees in line with the direction of your toes. By gently rotating your leg outward through your hip joint, you can explore how you can bend lower with your toes/knees pointing more outward, and how the movements become more challenging when you bring the toes/knees more inward with the feet parallel.

Many beginners arch the lower back and push their rear ends out when going into the Horse Stance. You will find the movement more comfortable, and more beneficial for your kidneys and lower back, if you tuck the rear in so your lower back is straight or slightly tucked in. This is also necessary in order to gain the energetic benefits.

Sixth Treasure:

Pumping the Water from the Origin of the Fountain - Bend forward and grab your ankles with your hands, with your fingers wrapping around the Achilles tendons. Ideally your thumbs are on the outside of the ankles, and your fingers touch the inside of the ankles. Look slightly forward so the flow of energy circulates freely through your throat and the front of your abdomen. The secret of this movement is to coordinate the strength of your breath with the action of your back and hands pulling up on your ankles to shift your weight. This coordinated action provides unusually powerful leverage. Vigorously inhale into your lower *tan tien*, filling your lower back and abdomen with air as you shift your weight slightly forward through the connection of your hands and Achilles tendons, to lever your body weight onto the balls of your feet. Exhale only after you fully land back on the ground. Gradually, both your breathing and the leveraging action of your ankles and feet will allow you to make little jumps like a frog. Don't force it, though; by practicing you will gradually find the "Origin of the Fountain."

Seventh Treasure:

The Tiger Grabs Its Prey - This movement comes from the lower *tan tien*, sometimes a hard thing for beginners to grasp. The body's momentum comes from pushing up from the feet and legs, with the energy directed through the waist.

Clench the Teeth, Widen the Eyes and Strike in the Four Directions - This movement usually requires additional practice. Start by breaking it down into small components, and doing it very slowly. To coordinate the gathering movement with the striking movement, use the waist to move the arms and then strike. The waist is the leader. Often people move the arms too far behind their bodies before the strike, so the movement is not well coordinated. This is a common mistake that, when corrected, really helps people perform the movement better.

People also inevitably use too much force when punching. They overstretch the arms and neglect the waist. Once again, waist movement is the key. Also, don't neglect the opposite arm that draws across the waist to counterbalance the extending fist. Remember to relax, not be frustrated, and practice it several times.

There is a child's game in which everyone holds hands to form a long line and the group starts moving from one end with everyone following like a whip or snake. The slightest swerving motion from the leader amplifies at the back of the line into a tremendous force. This movement acts in the same way. The waist is the leader that transmits the force from the legs out through the arms. Think of the instantaneous coiling and uncoiling of a snake when it strikes - that is like the expansion and release through this movement.

Be sure to clench the teeth and widen the eyes at the moment of each punch.

Eighth Treasure:
The White Crane Stretches Its Legs Behind and Forward
- Many beginners cannot maintain their balance for very long. It takes time to develop one's root. Focus your gaze on a distant object to help your balance. In the beginning, start your movement small, emphasizing balance over the height of your stretched leg. Bending the standing (weighted) leg slightly will also help your balance.

The White Crane Stretches Its Leg Behind - In the beginning, you can use the back of a chair to help you balance while you perform this movement. Some find it helpful to imagine that their feet are sinking in mud up to the ankles or focusing on the soles of the feet to feel a strong, rooted connection. It also helps to make sure that your lower back is straight, not arched backward, throughout the entire movement. Breathe deeply into your lower *tan tien*, making your whole body light, full of breath, and balanced over your leg, just like a crane. Rotate from the abdomen so your leg and upper body move together. When you have extended your leg behind, you can use images to help your balance. Imagine being a Crane with your standing leg and foot very firmly grounded.

The White Crane Stretches Its Leg Forward - Do not be discouraged! Most people cannot do this movement at first. Think about gradually improving your performance, with a sense of whole self and whole body coordination during the movement. In the beginning, you may want to stand between two chairs, using the back of each chair as a support as you bend down and rise up. This movement has a lot to do with developing a sense of the body moving back from the legs (as if you were going to sit on a stool, widening the lower back and allowing the tail bone to drop and connect with the ground and the perineum), while the leg stretches and extends forward and the hands extend. The back and the front of the body expanding opposition so you balance yourself as you bend and straighten the standing leg. This movement is more about balance and coordination of the whole body than about the strength of one leg. It is more important to maintain a sense of whole body movement and balance than it is to go all the way down without being able to rise.

Also students often raise their shoulders toward their ears as they attempt to go down. To avoid this, give up the idea of going down and replace it with the idea of backward and forward expansion. Focus on guiding your energy out through the center of your palms as well as maintaining a strong connection with the soles of your feet.

The White Crane Limbers Its Wings - Many people find the arm stretches of this section difficult. Imagine that your arms are large wings starting from your sternum (your sterno-clavicular joint) and extending outward through the joints of your shoulders, elbows, wrists, and hands all the way to the tips of your fingers. Gently extend your awareness to the tip of each finger when you move your arms (your wings). Do not tighten or overextend any joint. In this way, you allow maximum length through all of your arm structure and will gain more flexibility.

In the second section, when you fold one arm (one wing) over and back and the other arm under and back to join the hands, visualize your large wings unfolded, with your awareness extended to your fingertips (the tips of your feathers). As you fold your wings, let your fingertips lead the movement. In the beginning, if your fingers cannot reach far enough, you may use a small towel for your fingers to grab in the back. To circle the upper body in this posture, make sure you have a solid stance with some space between your legs, and initiate your body circle from your lower *tan tien*, letting your shoulders and arms move freely and easily. To conclude the movement, unfold your wings gently and gracefully, again letting the tips of your fingers initiate the opening of your arms (your wings). Always use the ebb and flow of your breath to support the development of each of your movements.

Water and Fire Meet
(Figure 45)

Chapter 5

Deepen Your Understanding

1

Guidelines to Increase the Effectiveness of Your Practice

Persistent practice is the first step to improvement and refinement of your Eight Treasures practice.

1. *Concentration of your spirit*: If your energy is scattered, your spirit will be scattered. The scattering of energy and spirit leads to ineffective cultivation. Focused cultivation, on the other hand, will help you concentrate and coordinate your energy and spirit. Gather your mind and concentrate on your movements.

2. *Mental tranquility*: When your mind is quiet and clear, your movement is graceful and the feeling of energy flow is obvious. Mental restlessness only causes stiff movement, congestion of energy flow, poor reflex response, and lack of awareness.

3. *Grounded and unhurried*: Grounded means your mind and body are subtle and quiet, not restless. Unhurried means your movements and breathing are not speedy or careless. The advanced stage of grounded and unhurried practice is effortless and responsive. As you practice at a grounded and unhurried pace, your movements and energy become light and effortless, gentle and responsive.

4. *Relaxed and thorough*: Your movements and breathing must be relaxed and continuous without stiffness, tension or hesitation.

5. *Avoid rigidity*: Each movement has *yin* and *yang* aspects of contraction and relaxation of body parts. There are movements with force and movements without force. Rigidity occurs by trying to use forceful power in every single part of a movement, or when the force is applied at the wrong time. The energy for force and the force itself come from inside; this is not muscular strength, but rather your internal *chi*.

6. *Natural*: All movements are natural. Use your waist/low back region as the axle of body movements. Never over-stretch, strain or force a movement. Avoid doing movements or postures in a way that feels unnatural to you.

7. *Balance*: Balance means synchronicity in breathing (inhaling and exhaling) and movement (retreat and advance). The center of the energy is in the lower *tan tien*. The energy is neither excessive nor deficient at the upper and lower extremities.

8. *Continuity*: All breathing is continuous without holding your breath. All movements are continuous without hesitation. Your energy is continuously changing from emptiness to fullness and from fullness to emptiness just like the *t'ai chi* of ever-changing *yin* and *yang*.

2
Learning About *Chi*

Eight Treasures practice stimulates and accelerates the circulation of bodily energy, or *chi*, to strengthen your bodily kingdom. The study of *chi* leads one to learn a great deal about life energy. Life energy manifests not just through your physical being, but through your mental and spiritual being as well. In fact, your physical, mental and spiritual energies are related and affect one another.

Scientists in China have studied spiritually achieved people using experiments that scientists in the United States would consider as being in the areas of parapsychology, psychic ability or ESP. One experiment to which I was exposed involved a child born with certain psychic abilities. The child, who was closely observed, was confined in a room containing only a chair and a table. An appointed person then drove twenty miles across town and wrote several words on a piece of paper, took this paper and the pen and put them in a safe and locked it. After the person returned to where the child was, he asked the child to recite what was written on the piece of paper. The child not only repeated the message orally, but also materialized the piece of paper and the pen! When they went back to the safe and opened it, they found that the paper and pen were gone.

This type of phenomenon is not exclusive to China. We hear about such things happening in different parts of the world. Some people are naturally born with similar abilities, but an expert *chi gong* practitioner may be able to perform similar feats. This means that such abilities can be cultivated. Achieved ones believe that everybody can develop and cultivate such abilities.

What is *Chi?*

In recent years, Chinese scientists have become fascinated with the phenomenon of *chi* which achieved masters have known about for thousands of years. What is this *chi?* It is the energy of nature that also exists in the human body.

A practitioner of *chi gong*, which is the study and mastery of *chi*, learns to use the mind to guide the *chi* to accomplish specific goals such as improved health. This mental guidance or imagery is carried by the *chi* to different locations in the body. For example, when a *chi gong* expert treats a patient, he can cause a change in the body's chemistry and make a paralyzed leg move. This can happen regardless of whether or not the patient believes that it can work. Is it possible then that the *chi* emitted by the practitioner causes not just physical but an intelligent response from the recipient's body?

Recently in China, trained researchers and physicists have been doing a lot of research in the area of *chi*. "What is *chi?*" is the question they are trying to answer. The emission of *chi* by *chi gong* experts has been measured and documented. Numerous experiments were conducted which demonstrated that *chi*, as measured from a person's hands, consists of various frequencies of near infrared radiation, electromagnetic fields, heat, light and micro-particles. The *chi* was measured while being emitted and projected from accomplished *chi* masters. When measured on an instrument, they found that this emission differed slightly in wave patterns from one master to another.

While attempting to identify this *chi*, Chinese scientists have concluded that this so-called *chi* really contains two aspects: 1) an informational message, and 2) the substance/carrier of this information.

An example is easily illustrated by the transmission of images or data over telephone lines, where on the receiving end, an instrument interprets signals that are merely different impulses or waves back into data and images. So the carrier is the electrical or light impulse and waves and the information is the variation of these impulses and waves that were purposely programmed at the beginning of transmission.

The scientific speculation that *chi* is composed of these two aspects and that it circulates through the human body is a different way of explaining the ancient concept of energy circulation and its effects on specific organs and parts of the body. Those of you who are trying to intellectualize and understand the composition of *chi* may find this helpful.

In the West, recent works by pioneers in the field of psychobiological science have led to the postulation that emotion can be stored in different parts of bodily tissues, muscles and fat. Thus when considering the concept of *chi,* it can be understood that when a person loses pounds of fat, he or she might start reexperiencing some trauma experienced in the past. Also, specialized body work such as deep tissue massage can elicit an emotional response such as sadness or fear, or placing acupuncture needles on certain points can bring recall of a scene from a dramatic situation, for example a childhood trauma 30 years ago.

Chi is All-Encompassing
Let me explain the concept of *chi*. I do not want you to limit your mind to thinking about *chi* as only being present in *chi gong* exercises, Eight Treasures and other internal arts. Thought is a manifestation of *chi*, emotion is *chi* and action is *chi*. The cultivation of *chi* is very broad and should not be conceptually limited to physical health practices.

This broader concept of *chi* is very exciting. What you are cultivating is something that not only benefits you in terms of health but will also benefit you at much deeper levels of your psyche and spirit. Practitioners of the Integral Way seek to eventually achieve oneness with universal being. This can be accomplished by changing yourself internally if you have the ability to maintain the flow of *chi*.

Have you ever wondered how people can be healed by *chi gong* healing, acupuncture treatments or laying-on of hands? Acupuncture needles are consciously applied to reorganize the *chi* of a patient's body, or a healer's hands can emit *chi*. In either case, the physiological *chi* brings healing to the diseased or unbalanced person through a conscious programmed message from the practitioner.

In our daily lives, we witness the power of our own minds to make things happen by affecting *chi*. One example is changing our body functions, as in biofeedback. So then, if you are well versed and disciplined in the mastery of *chi*, would it not be conceivable that you can begin to work on naturally changing this energy? It is not only possible, it has been done by the developed ones in the high mountains of China.

What does "maintain the flow of *chi*" mean? It metaphorically describes internal energy circulation. It means being connected and in synchrony with all elements inside your being and with all things outside of your being. It takes you to a state of oneness. Oneness or integralness of life is a hard concept to grasp; it means "not separate," or "to become the universe." In time, through spiritual evolution, you become aware that you can go on in continual, never-ending life, just like the perpetual motion of the universe. Your body, which consists of *chi*, *shen* (spirit) and *jing*[3] (essence), will continue to function naturally so you can become one with the universe, as the ancient developed ones described.

Have you wondered how ancient masters could know what was happening in the world without leaving their mountain retreat? From a modern scientific point of view, this is impossible because of the lack of physical communication. Yet in ancient times, achieved masters who practiced special cultivation could know who was going to appear at their door and what was happening in the world.

Chi, *shen* and *jing* are interrelated. The function of the *shen* is to guide one's life. Without *shen,* the *chi* will lose all sense of direction. *Chi* can be developed from the *jing*, and the refinement of *chi* also supports *shen.*

Pre-Natal and Post-Natal *Chi*
Each person needs both pre-natal and post-natal *chi* (energy) to survive.

We are born with pre-natal *or* ancestral *chi*, which is sometimes called pre-Heaven *chi*, or *xian tien zhi chi* in Chinese. Pre-natal *chi* encompasses *jing*, matter, and potential. *Jing* is the substantive essence that you inherit that determines your intellectual and physical potential. From the western point of view, *jing* could be equated with genetics. Pre-natal *chi* originates through the union of the sperm and egg; it comes from our parents and from heavenly and earthly energies. From the ancient point of view, how much reproductive potential and essence you have depends upon how

---

[3] *Jing* is sometimes spelled *tsing* or *ching*.

much *jing* you have. *Jing* is stored energy in the body; specifically, it is stored in the kidneys.

The common view holds that *jing* cannot be replenished if it
becomes lost or weakened. The masters, however, believe that
jing can be replenished as well as refined through the internal arts
of cultivation. Such activity slows the aging process and results in
longevity. Our interest in practicing the Eight Treasures is to change
and refine *jing*.

For example, if you are bald due to a genetic tendency, you
were genetically programmed to be bald. However, according to
ancient masters, certain genetic programming can be changed by
refining your pre-natal *chi*. Different levels of attainment require
different levels of dedication and practice. There were many
instances in history where practitioners over 70 years of age
replaced an old set of teeth with new teeth by cultivation. You
may wonder how long you would have to practice the Eight
Treasures every day before you could start to change your genetic
destiny. No general estimate is available; however, with persistence,
anything is possible as long as the environment supports the change.
This is a personal challenge.

The Eight Treasures does not claim to cure baldness or grow
new teeth, but it will improve your health and longevity. The
Eight Treasures can serve as stepping stones to any level of attainment to which you aspire. The purpose of cultivation is not only
longevity, but to be able to live life to the fullest and fulfill our
divine nature.

Post-natal *chi* is also called after-Heaven *chi* or acquired *chi*. It
is derived from digestion and absorption, mainly when the stomach
and spleen-pancreas transform food into nutritive *chi*. Post-natal
chi is much easier to manage by the mind. To obtain nutritive *chi*,
you must have good digestion and eat nutritious food.

Post-natal *chi* also comes from air. In the body, nutrients from
high quality foods combined with good air produce precious post-
natal *chi*. Good digestion and respiration are essential for this
process. The Eight Treasures can help you develop and practice
good respiration and help stimulate digestion.

Chi and Your Genetic Potential

Modern science has brought many benefits to human life. However, it has also brought up questions of an ethical nature, particularly new advancements in genetic engineering. Almost every day when I read the paper, I see another advancement, such as scientists mapping out a gene that causes alcoholism, a gene that causes colon cancer, and even a gene that may relate to longevity. The genetic information within each individual collectively makes up our genetic destination. Such genetic information might determine how long you are going to live, what illnesses you will develop or become susceptible to, and your physical and intellectual capabilities. Modern science might use this understanding to manipulate the quality or information contained within specific genes. Thus it is conceivable that some day you can go to a lab and tell your physician or scientist that you want to live hundreds of years, and they will then change your genes to program you so you can do that. This is an interesting thought.

But what are the ethical consequences of someone who uses their energy negatively to harm others, living to be 150 years old? Have we explored our genetic benefit or disbenefit to ourselves, each individual person? Are we prepared to live beyond our genetic destination? There are physical, psychological and spiritual considerations. If a person is miserable or lives without purpose, would an extra 50 years improve the quality of their present existence, or would it simply add more confusion and suffering? Think about it. Altering our human genetic destiny is a new possibility that we have no idea how to deal with at a conventional level.

Earlier we talked about the Eight Treasures and its effects when working on and refining the pre-natal aspect of your being. Pre-natal *chi* is stored in the eight extraordinary channels, and by refining the *chi* within them, you can change a pre-destined pre-natal plan. This may also be an attempt of humankind to have control over nature. The approach of the scientific community is an interesting one; however, changing one thing out of context is partial and limited, because unanticipated imbalances will occur. Rather than relying on scientific advances for salvation, I suggest you achieve mastery of yourself, through your own sincerity, discipline and correct motivation.

The ancient achieved ones had a similar idea about changing their genetic destiny, but instead of opening and dissecting bodies to find a gene and change it, they adopted a natural way that caused very little disturbance to society at large or to themselves individually. The ancient developed ones aspired to live forever, but their immortality was not limited to either the physical or the spiritual realm. It has been known in China that there were great masters who physically lived to be 800 years old. Peng Zhu, for example, was such a person. Such people appeared generation after generation and could be seen in physical form interacting with people.

When healing modalities of Chinese medicine are used on people who are not self-motivated in cultivation, it is impossible for their *jing* to be changed. In other words, for many people, *jing* can never be replenished. But for those who take an active role in their own cultivation, a change can definitely happen. Earlier I quoted the example of developed ones who experienced a new set of teeth at age 70; they also restored their whole head of black hair, and had the ability to procreate. All these are reversals of genetic coding.

3
Chi or Energy Aspects of the Eight Treasures

Learn the Form, Then Go Beyond
Ordinarily, people look for external things to imitate and learn, and they insist that a form needs to be done in a certain way. However, the purpose of doing this exercise is not merely to be able to do or perform the form, but to attain something that is not formed. You may master the form, but the form does not stay the same during your whole life, because you make progress. As you attain a certain degree of accomplishment, you move to another, higher level.

Certainly, without a form, there would be no way to teach, but a form should not become limited and rigid. The purpose of the Eight Treasures and all the gentle styles of movement that we teach is not merely to achieve a certain standard of external movement and physical control as in sports and dance. Through experiencing the validity of the subtle universal law, you can realize its power to transform your life. By subtle universal law, I am referring to the principle of energy correspondence, and the natural truths of life you learn through following the Integral Way. By balancing your own internal energies and applying the natural laws discovered through this type of practice in daily life, a harmonious response from the universe occurs naturally.

How *Chi* Moves

A universal principle revealed in *t'ai chi* movement is that sudden movement causes energy to stagnate, while gentle, rhythmic movement brings about the flow of energy. Sudden movement must always stop quickly; inevitably there is a pause and the energy flow is inhibited. Similarly, hasty action ultimately results in slowness because it quickly exhausts your energy, while gentle, rhythmic movement can be continued with great endurance. With this logic, we can understand that those who are violent can afford only one show of force at a time, thus, in reality they are weak.

Thus, in practicing the Eight Treasures, all movements are grounded and unhurried, relaxed and thorough, and continuous.

Yin and *Yang*

Understanding the *yin-yang* system provides a basis for the analysis of all phenomena into complementary aspects. The universe has two general aspects or categories called *yin* and *yang*. Where there is one pole, there must also be another. *Yin* and *yang* have no fixed definition, which makes the terms virtually untranslatable. They represent two broad categories of complements, which include the correspondences of receding and proceeding, negative and positive, inert and active, gross and subtle, form and action, actual and potential. The qualities of *yin* and *yang* are relative, not absolute.

When *yin* and *yang* come together, there is life: an organism, a balance. The *yin* aspect of a person is the material and substantial; the *yang* aspect is the functional. The union of *yin* and *yang* in individual life enables you to achieve higher things. We all have inherent components, and refining them brings out the full potential of an individual's life.

All movements of the Eight Treasures have the two opposing (and complementary) aspects, which are *yin* and *yang*. Some movements are also paired in a *yin* and *yang* sequence or vice versa. The basic concepts of *yin* and *yang* as applied to the physical exercises of the Eight Treasures and their corresponding energy flow are:

Yin: receptive/relaxing, placid, contracting, inward and downward
    Yang: active, swift, expanding, outward and upward

Another way to look at the two aspects of energy movement are:

Yin: lower, deep, front circulation
Yang: higher, surface, back circulation

Below is the *T'ai Chi* Symbol. It represents balance, "oneness" of *yin* and *yang,* and the secret of longevity. *Yin* is represented by the dark side of the circle and *yang* by the light side.

T'ai Chi **Symbol**

Figure 46

Next is the same figure with markings that indicate the *yin* and *yang* aspects of the energetic cycle of a 24-hour period.

The Daily Cycle of *Yin* and *Yang*

Figure 47

You can use the alternation of *yin* and *yang* as a clue to nature's cycle of day and night. At midnight, *yang* energy begins to rise. *Yang* energy increases at 6 a.m. *Yang* energy peaks and begins to be exhausted at noon (pure *yang*); *yin* begins at this time. *Yin* increases at 6:00 p.m. and peaks at midnight. At midnight, *yang* begins to rise again.

We can apply the understanding of this energy cycle to our lives. Beginning at midnight, the energy of the body begins to rise and move upward and outward, becoming active from the static *yin* state. By noon, the energy has reached the highest point of the body (the head) and is characterized by activities and functions of the sun at high noon. At noon, you should start to prepare for the waning and winding down of energy by quieting your mind as your energy descends downward, inward and becomes static as midnight approaches. Hence, after the sun goes down, you should be quiet, passive and inactive until after midnight, when the *yang* part of the cycle resumes. Staying in tune with nature's cycles will enhance your vitality and increase your spiritual clarity.

The Three *Tan Tien*

The three *tan tien* function as the three main energy centers of a human body. A *tan tien* is an internal energy center of a specific region. In modern terms, it could be called a nerve center.

The upper *tan tien* is located inside the central point between the eyebrows. The middle *tan tien* is located inside the center of the chest. The lower *tan tien* is located inside the lower abdomen. The following figure shows the location of the *tan tien:*

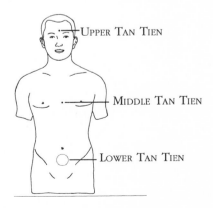

Figure 48

The term *tan tien* translates as "field of elixir," and refers more to an area than a point. These major energy storage areas of the body provide energy for the various expressions of one's being, specifically the intellectual, emotional and sexual aspects, which correspond to the upper, middle and lower *tan tien*, respectively. However, the energy stored in each of these locations can be refined through cultivation without indulging in these expressions.

As a rule, women are advised to keep their energy centered in the middle *tan tien*. This is because a woman's natural center is already low. For most people, especially women and young men (due to the strength of sexual energy associated with the lower *tan tien*), the middle *tan tien* is the right, safe spot to pay attention to and cultivate. Thus after you finish practicing the Eight Treasures, and at other times of the day, you may wish to focus your energy at the heart center or middle *tan tien*.

People who are physically weak or aging fast will benefit from more vitality. Exercise increases vitality, and cultivation of energy in the lower *tan tien* assists in rejuvenation.

Certain styles of *chi gong* exercise emphasize different aspects or parts of the body. The Eight Treasures work not only on all parts of the body, but also activate all twelve organ-system channels and the eight extraordinary channels. Thus the Eight Treasures work with all three *tan tien* as part of an integral, complete practice.

The Eight Treasures is an Internal Practice

The Eight Treasures can be practiced on several levels. The first level is therapeutic, for health and well-being. At this level, the practice unblocks stagnant energy and improves the circulation of *chi*. This level also helps people with a physical problem to restore some degree of normal health. Another level is that of martial arts, although we do not teach or promote fighting. Gaining mastery over yourself is more important than attempting to control other people. After all, if you do not have mastery over yourself, then who or what controls you?

> *Fighting to win*
> *   is very limited.*
> *If you quit trying to fight and win,*
> *   and enjoy practicing for nothing,*
> *   then you attain the naturalness of the art.*

The more advanced level is for those who wish to practice to prevent illness, maintain health, and enhance their vitality, internally and externally. This level can be refined further for physical and genetic transformation.

This third level and those above are spiritual practices that concern positive energy, transformation, and rearrangement. This takes place on the subtle level instead of the visible level. Spiritual practice may have a particular purpose such as developing a good mind, opening your wisdom, increasing memory power, or uplifting yourself to a different level of existence. The highest level of practice is an alchemical process leading to spiritual attainment and the achievement of immortality.

The Tiger Grabs Its Prey
(Figure 49)

Chapter 6

The Origin of the Eight Treasures

Commentary by Hua-Ching Ni

The Eight Treasures, which is a form of *dao-in*, has been passed down for a very long time. Different records indicate the Eight Treasures is at least six thousand years old.

In the esoteric spiritual heritage, the Eight Treasures are called *"Pa Kun Dao-In."* *Pa* means eight, *Kun* means respected old men, *Dao* means conducting, and *In* means channelling. All together, they convey the meaning: "channelling exercises for your bodily energy from the eight achieved ones."

From the Warring Period which began around 403 B.C.E. through the Ching dynasty (248-207 B.C.E.) and up to the Han Dynasty (206 B.C.E. - 219 C.E.), many people were considered "Scholars of Formulas and Methods." Today, we would say that the Scholars of Formulas and Methods were experts or specialists who took a scientific approach to life. They preserved useful methods of living that had been developed prior to their time. However, because there was no protection for their special knowledge or skill, these methods became personal or family secrets. The methods that were passed along to the other students may not have been complete, which was a great loss.

I would like to tell you the legend of Prince Liu Ahn. As a modern student you must take this legend with a grain of salt, although we should remain objective toward all documentary records.

During the Han Dynasty, Huai Nan Zi (active around 170-86 B.C.E.), who was also called Prince Liu Ahn, seriously pursued spiritual immortality. Because he was so enthusiastic, he invited the most highly achieved ones, a team of eight respected older individuals, to become his teachers. Nobody knew their real age, so people just called them the eight old achieved ones.

The Prince was not an ordinary fellow; he had great wealth to invite good teachers. Despite wealth, however, finding a good teacher still depends on the student's dedication and sincerity. Based on one's spiritual sincerity, one may attract the attention of real achieved ones. However, one must be careful; surely one is vulnerable to offers from false teachings, too.

When the eight achieved ones came to visit the Prince, the gatekeeper gave them trouble. He told them, "Our prince is interested in learning from people who never become old, people who live as long as they wish, and who know all the depth that all scholars in the world can achieve. He is also interested in people who are brave, who have the physical strength to raise heavy objects and who are not afraid of death. However, you are older people and you speak like you are uneducated. How can our prince be interested in you? As far as I can see, you do not know anything, so how could you know the profound truth of life? If you are only looking for a good time here, you had better forget it, because you will not find it. I dare not inform our prince that you are here, because I will be scolded for receiving common old people like you who could come from any village."

The eight old ones laughed and said, "We came because we heard the prince admires virtuous, developed people, and that he never tires of studying. We heard that anyone who has even a small amount of achievement comes to see him.

"Do you not know that in ancient times, the wise Prince Meng Chang Jun welcomed people whose achievement was small, like knowing the multiplication table or having the ability to imitate a dog bark or rooster crow? He welcomed all such people as guests. Later, when the prince lost the favor of the king and had to escape, it was these people who assisted him and saved his life.

"Do you not know that when another king eagerly wished to obtain the fastest horses in the world, he took the advice of one of his advisors? The advisor went out and in the name of the king, paid a thousand silver coins for the bones of a dead horse that was known to have been very fast. Because of that, people from all around knew that the king greatly valued fast horses, and soon the best ones were being brought to the palace to sell to him.

"Although we are ordinary and humble, we came because we feel that your prince is wise and strong. What he has already gathered and learned are the bones of a dead horse, not real horses. We are the real ones he wishes to learn from."

The gate officer replied, "I do not say you were not fast horses many years ago, but now all of you are worn out and have become too old."

"That is no matter," the old men said. "If you feel we are too old to help the prince, then we will come back to see you when we grow younger. It seems your prince is only interested in young people, not old people, so when we grow younger, we will come back."

Just after saying this, the vision of the gate officer suddenly changed, and he saw them as nicely dressed young men around 15 to 18 years old. This startled the gate officer, and he rushed in to tell the prince what had happened. The prince did not even take time to put his shoes on correctly; he immediately went outside to greet them, and brought them into the middle hall and gave them comfortable seats. They received his salutation surrounded by the sweet fragrance of incense (at that time incense was just small pieces of fragrant wood burning in a small cauldron). The prince became a humble, receptive student with great enthusiasm to learn from them.

This is the beginning of the legend. I hesitate to continue, because if I do it may only encourage you to become an ordinary follower of religious Taoism. All religions are misapplications of the mind; they block the ability of people to take responsibility in all aspects of life The natural universal spirit is suitably manifested in a constructive everyday life. No religion can replace self-respect and self-responsibility. All people are similarly endowed with a body, mind, and spirit, but unless a person lives correctly, there is no extra help from nature or God.

As a young man, Prince Liu Ahn had excelled in his studies, including Confucianism and special skills like secret magic. His research was never open to the public, but he wrote two books which he gave to society.

Huai Nan Zi (Tzu) (淮南子), the book of Prince Liu Ahn has two parts. The first part, the popularly known *Huai Nan Zi,* is a philosophical discussion. The published version contained 21 chapters. Sections of it have been translated into English. The second part is called *The 10,000 Great Treasures* (萬年鴻寶). In this part, Liu Ahn discusses the method of internal alchemy, immortality and instant bodily transformation, and invisibility and restoration. This is the knowledge he obtained from the Eight Immortals.

It seems that Liu Ahn wrote the first part, *Huai Nan Zi,* before he met the eight respected older ones. He had attained some degree of spiritual achievement, but not to any great depth. The scope of *Huai Nan Zi* is much more encompassing than that of any other Chinese spiritual classic, so it can be considered an important book.

The 10,000 Great Treasures is a record of the teachings of the eight achieved masters who were known as the Eight Seniors of

Huai Nan (south of the river of Huai). It is the work of many, while *Bao Po Tzu*[4] is the work of only one individual. *Treasure for 10,000 Years* consisted of three volumes or parts. At that time, magic practice still existed, and a developed individual could physically transform before your eyes. This achievement was real, and throughout the centuries, people have appeared who can do such things.

Huai Nan Zi still exists, but *The 10,000 Great Treasures* has been lost because it was hidden by people who were either selfish or concerned for the public safety. We know of its existence from references in other records. A student's character usually must be tested for many lifetimes to be prepared to learn these practices. I have not met anyone who could pass the test. This is due to the loss of the spiritual aspect of human development. Magic was not passed down to people during the time of my youth, or if it was, I must have failed the test of my own teachers. Learning it, or just thinking about learning it, can make your mind wild, because you can get anything you want instantly. Perhaps because of my nature, my teachers only taught me those things that take a long time to achieve, but have lasting value. They knew the world well and knew me well. Today, as I reflect upon the matter, I think my teachers were right. I am grateful to enjoy the hard way of life and achievement.

Prince Liu Ahn's books were substantial due to his profound practice, unlike modern books on Taoist philosophy, written by people who have not achieved real practice and are merely scholarly in nature. Scholars can only superficially understand Prince Liu Ahn's books because ancient natural knowledge cannot be completely conveyed in language. I have seen various versions of *Huai Nan Zi*, in English but they only touched upon the philosophy.

The purpose of the Eight Treasures is to give people a good

---

[4]In order to avoid confusion about the Chinese books, *Bao Po Tzu* is the book of Kou Hong who was active from 265 to 419 C.E. (See my work *Life and Teaching of Two Immortals, Volume I*). *Bao Po Tzu* has two parts. Part one or the *External Book* discusses society and government. It was his study of the ancient learning which he selected and integrated. Part two or the *Internal Book* talks about the possibility and the practice of immortality, which has been literally translated by scholars. My impression of the translations is that they may only have touched upon the general level. If you learn from a Chinese scholar or Taoist priest, be aware that their shamanistic practice is not the same as the scientific approach of Kou Hong. The scholars and priests make nature as God, which is not a subject for research. Kou Hong accepted nature as nature, which can be an object for research and cultivation as to how it serves you best. Human life is small; it is a small model of the complete self-nature of the universe, its big model.

foundation of health. We cannot assume that if you practice them you will achieve instant physical transformation, but at least, the practice can keep you younger and healthier.

Q: Did the old achieved ones teach the prince to do the Eight Treasures?

Master Ni: *Dao-in*, including the Eight Treasures, was one part of their practice. That was a time when the first stage of chemistry developed to a high peak. The purpose of that chemistry was magic and medicine; alchemy was for immortality. Naturally Prince Liu Ahn had the position and the financial power to gather valuable materials for that purpose and put it into practice.

There are several records that describe Liu Ahn's fate. One simply says that he achieved himself. Another states that he was feared by Emperor Wu of the Han dynasty, who was Prince Liu Ahn's nephew. Emperor Wu (108-86 B.C.E.) accepted the advice of a Confucian scholar to combine Confucius' teaching with the teachings of other schools such as the School of *Yin* and *Yang* in order to support the tyrannical ruling system. I have talked about Emperor Wu in one of my other books. He frantically pursued physical immortality.

Liu Ahn gathered many developed people around him, but the young emperor felt that perhaps Liu Ahn was building a power base to eventually replace him, so he ordered his arrest. Another record says that when the whole family was arrested, Liu Ahn's refinement process was all accomplished. So when Emperor Wu began to persecute Liu Ahn and his family, they all swallowed the immortal medicine and disappeared.

I believe that the second record is correct, because the emperor, who witnessed the achievement of his uncle, suddenly developed a strong interest in the pursuit of immortality.

That legend about Liu Ahn says that the whole family ate some kind of elixir and then achieved. In my books, I present that immortal alchemy as an individual process of combining internal spiritual energies, not a physical process of combining herbal substances that can be eaten.

A third record just says that the prince suffered the punishment when the emperor arrested him. I do not accept this, because if Liu Ahn failed, there was nothing to support Emperor Wu's subsequent interest in such a pursuit.

Emperor Wu believed that because he was emperor, he was much more powerful than his uncle, and thus could have more developed teachers and material to support his pursuit. However, he was overconfident that he would be able to achieve whatever he wanted; the real teachers all stayed hidden from him.

In ancient times, if a person wished to achieve immortality, he had to pray to the Goddess of West Pond for protection, help and inspiration. She was an ancient achieved woman. Nobody really knew when she achieved herself; there were some legends, but we cannot know if they were accurate. Nevertheless, she was the teacher of all immortal people at that time. Whoever wished to achieve immortality, especially men, had to bow to her. This has metaphoric meaning, but realistically, there is such a goddess.

Emperor Wu killed many animals and collected many valuables as an offering to the Goddess of West Pond. After many years, the goddess responded by sending the Lady of Upper Sphere to him. To my surprise, this interview was described as a personal interview, not a vision, dream or trance. I believe that no highly achieved spiritual being would be willing to meet an emperor whose body was desirous and whose mind was ambitious, yet Emperor Wu truly witnessed the real presence of the Lady of Upper Sphere. She looked like a maiden around 15 or 16 years old; she was extraordinarily beautiful but not weak.

She talked to Emperor Wu in a straightforward manner that all manly men admired at that time. She asked, "Are you really interested in learning Tao? You have been looking very diligently for it, but you cannot find it. There is a reason; do you know what it is? You are tyrannical and you indulge in sex. You surround yourself with luxury, decadence and waste. You create burdens for people, and you are cruel and destructive. Immortality is energy; if you wish to cultivate yourself, first you must regulate your mind. If you wish to regulate your mind, your must first correct your temperament. If you continue to be cruel, your energy will undermine your spirit; thus your spirit will suffer disturbance, become inactive and cannot help you.

"Your indulgence in sex is wearing out your soul. If your internal physical essence is empty, then your soul becomes dissolute. Because of constant decadence, your interests are multiple and confused, thus, your physical essence is contaminated. If you continue this way, your physical life will wither and your soul can only sink.

"You are cold blooded and unkind. Because you have lost the kindness of your true nature and become cruel, your vision has been lost. You are destructive, jealous and suspicious, so your mind is always in conflict, thus your internal fluid does not support you or flow naturally. Internally you worry, so externally you are isolated from the good energy.

"This behavior is like knives and swords that cut you to pieces. Although you think you are interested in living an eternal life, if you cannot eliminate these difficulties, you will keep requesting the attention of the immortal realm but in the end there will be no fruit for you." That was the warning the Lady of Upper Sphere gave to Emperor Wu.

My comment is that there are two types of student. One type pays attention to what causes the pursuit of immortality to fail and what is realistic. Such a student learns to achieve oneself without much difficulty, mistake or trouble. The other type of student sees how much Emperor Wu enjoyed, how many women he had, how many wars he fought, how much killing he had done and how much worldly glory he had, but he would not give up one bit of worldly indulgence to achieve immortality.

From Emperor Wu's time on, the divergence in learning Tao widened. Some were still serious about keeping all the necessary disciplines in order to achieve themselves. Others, who had minds like Emperor Wu, developed the indulgent mentality of folk Taoism. Emperor Wu was one of the early founders of Taoist religion. There is a big market for this type of "immortal pursuit" which is not truthful spiritual learning and teaching. So from there came the division between pure esoteric spiritual practice and worldly folk Taoism. One water is clean and clear, while the other is polluted.

I do not have anything more to say about folk religion, but in the future, as the West becomes more open to multiple cultures, it will face the same problem of having to choose between the two. I do not reject fantasy; a little bit is all right, because people's stages are different. However, if you treat fantasy as if it were truth, you can never attain Tao.

Q: Were the eight respected ones who taught Prince Liu Ahn the Eight Treasures the same as the Eight Immortals?

Master Ni: Those eight respected ones came much earlier than the Eight Immortals of later religious promotion. Those eight masters (seven men, one woman) lived in different generations and different times.[5] Surely immortals can be together, but that picture is a fantasy. The eight achieved ones and the Eight Immortals of religious promotion are two different groups of people.

Dao-In was the early physical art of immortality, as far back as Fu Shi (3582-2738 B.C.E.).

Q: Did Liu Ahn practice the Eight Treasures and become strong?

Master Ni: Liu Ahn surely attained the great collection of the ancient arts. Dao-in is one of them. So the Eight Treasures is called Pa (Eight) Kun (respected old one) Dao-In because of the source. People all know that everyone has a body and a mind, but few people know they have a spirit. Most are ignorant of the fact that the body is the foundation, the mind is the function, and the spirit is the guiding energy. Once the direction of the function, your mind, is set, then you need energy for accomplishment. If your mind goes in the wrong direction, you will waste your spiritual energy and also destroy your life foundation. That is really very simple.

In learning the Integral Way, which I do *not* call Taoism, when you live in the world, you must be upright. You are a king or queen of the numerous life beings within you. You are the leader and are responsible for all of your tiny partners. If you are wise and just, then your life is peaceful and orderly. It is the same thing as social leadership. The leadership of your life must be correct for your life. So first you need to learn the natural principles of life. In my book, *The Esoteric Tao Teh Ching*, Lao Tzu teaches the way to govern your own body kingdom. With that healthy foundation, you can utilize your energy to move in the right direction. By practicing Eight Treasures *dao-in* you can make the necessary alignment, strengthen your bodily kingdom, and gather and refine your energy to develop yourself.

---

[5]Hua-Ching Ni is referring to very popular and beautiful Chinese religious works of art depicting the Eight Immortals. Usually they are sitting together on a boat in the wavy ocean.

Section 4
Advanced Practice

At the advanced level, the focus is on learning more about chi *in your practice, on self-cultivation as part of a healthy life, on improving all aspects of your lifestyle, and on virtuous fulfillment as part of self-cultivation. You move from the formed to the unformed, from learning the movement to learning something unmoved, from the complicated to the simple, and from multiplicity to oneness.*

The Weeping Willow Shivers in the Early Morning Breeze
(Figure 50)

Chapter 7

The Secrets of Advanced Practice

1
The Eight Treasures as a Foundation

The Eight Treasures is an appropriate practice for all stages of spiritual self-cultivation. It is a type of *chi gong*, which means energy discipline. After learning the Eight Treasures, one can then master other types of *chi gong* such as *t'ai chi* movement.

Certain styles of *chi gong* emphasize all aspects or all parts of the body. The Eight Treasures is one such complete system. (The 64-movement version of the Eight Treasures gives additional details, but the 32-movement version we teach is still complete.) The Eight Treasures works not only on the entire body, but also activates all 12 regular channels and the eight extraordinary channels (sometimes called meridians). Other *chi gong* styles may activate only specific channels.

The Eight Treasures provides a combination of breathing and energy guidance techniques that open all major channels of the body (including both the regular channels and the extraordinary channels) and allow the gathering of your own energy and the subtle energy in your environment. It is the first form in our series of five and is specifically designed to tonify, stretch and reshape the body. It provides a secure foundation for further internal work and self-cultivation.

2
Complete Cultivation

There are two main aspects of cultivation. The first is internal cultivation, which consists of practicing methods and techniques of cultivation. The second aspect is external cultivation, which is living and practicing virtue in your life. Your development and cultivation will be incomplete if you lack either of these. The ultimate goal of continual evolution is to achieve oneness with the universe or eternity. All spiritual traditions have a concept of eternity that includes Heaven or the universe in a broader sense.

There are three aspects of being human: *jing*, *chi* and *shen*. *Jing* is essence or genetic potential, *chi* is the mobilizing function and *shen* is the guiding spirit. In order to accomplish the goal of oneness with the universe, we must actively work on all three of these aspects or spheres by participating in the deep eternal flow of universal life.

How Eight Treasures and Self-Cultivation Go Together

In ancient times, *dao-in* was considered immortal practice. It may have been the only practice or method recognized by common people of ancient times. I believe that there were not many complicated spiritual practices, only disciplines such as using herbs and maintaining personal sexual energy for higher transformation or sublimation. During the first stage of human existence, there were not many mental problems to plague people, unlike today when people are burdened by their overdeveloped minds.

As a function of life, the mind can be either positive or negative, depending upon how it is managed. Psychological attitudes did not trouble ancient people, because they lived naturally and accepted things naturally. They did not need to think a lot or make many choices or do intellectual work to earn a living.

The mind is subtle, but the spiritual level is much more subtle. Such energy may be subtle, but it is powerful. It is said that "Thoughts are as loud as thunder." If you think incorrectly, it can lead to misconduct. Instead you can use your thoughts to lead you to a positive result, such as having a healthy life. Mental discipline or internal discipline is actually more important than external disciplines. You need to guard yourself not only externally from temptation, but also internally from negative or improper thoughts. A healthy life and healthy mind can be cultivated through good practices that strengthen your whole life.

When most people describe their spiritual experiences, what they talk about is almost always related to their experience of their own body or psychology rather than spiritual reality. Spiritual reality is something you accomplish during your life process. Once you are born into the world, you continue to shape yourself. If you are looking for immortality or spiritual survival after death, life is not an event or a concept or anything you can point to.

Spiritual evolution means starting from the physical level to become a high spiritual being, which is the result of your own development or personal creation. A spiritual being converges multiple light particles as its body. In other words, a spiritual being has a light body. Immortality is a matter of becoming pure energy. People should value the opportunity that life offers to purify their energy internally and externally. Mistakes can be extremely costly, because although the span of life is not long, the suffering of the soul afterward can be very long indeed.

Spiritual development is a long journey. Learning energy movement such as the Eight Treasures is one good way to start on the path of self-deliverance.

Cultivation of the Higher Esoteric Science of Spirituality: Do It Completely or Don't Do It At All

The Eight Treasures can be practiced with various objectives. Most people wish to derive health benefits from the practice. However, those who decide to use it as a stepping stone to further their spiritual objectives would do well to heed a basic principle: regard your *chi* as if it were a matter of life and death. The contamination of *chi* is that serious. If you are committed to cultivating yourself, you must take your spiritual refinement seriously. If you are not serious, then don't do it at all, and just practice the Eight Treasures for health, adopting the wisdom of this tradition to help you live an effective, joyous life. This is because as you cultivate yourself, the impacts of negativity on your life will be *magnified* tremendously, compared to how it would affect an ordinary person.

Q: I don't understand. If one cultivates oneself, won't any negative impact be the same? Please explain.

A: The impact will be greater, because as you cultivate yourself, your body becomes more open and your being becomes like a big pond. If you have one poisonous thought, the damage will spread throughout your entire being; when your channels were not as open, the potential for damage was limited. This is why the natural spiritual tradition has been kept a secret.

Thus if you do it, do it completely. Otherwise, you should not pursue it at all.

Spiritual self-cultivation is a serious responsibility. The potential for damage is great. If you wish to go beyond genetic destiny by changing your *jing* (pre-natal inclination) at a much higher alchemical level, that is when cultivation has the potential to become dangerous, destructive or crumble your whole foundation of life. But once you pass a certain point or tests in your cultivation, refinement and development, then natural abilities come to you, such as psychic abilities. When this happens, you transcend the concept of time; you can be in the past, present and future at the same time, receiving information. That is how the ancient achieved ones could know the past and future and communicate with one another without leaving their mountain huts.

The beneficial aspects of *t'ai chi* exercise, *chi gong*, and Eight Treasures come through earnest practice and living a virtuous life, and are not dangerous in any way whatsoever. They are decidedly helpful and positive.

3
Go Deeper into Eight Treasures

The Eight Treasures are designed to harvest and store post- and pre-natal *chi*. In order to fully benefit from these movements, you must understand *chi* so you can store it. This practice is like opening up a savings account to effectively accumulate life energy. You can save *chi* and then withdraw it in times of need.

All of the Eight Treasures stimulate the kidneys, which are the root of your vital energy storage tank. Stimulation of the kidneys has the same effect as turning the soil over when cultivating plants in a garden. Each movement has a *yin* and a *yang* aspect, thus there is an interplay between *yin* and *yang* energy in the body.

The next section will cover basic theories of energy movement, especially the twelve channels and the eight extraordinary channels. It is important for a practitioner of the Eight Treasures to know the twelve channels, their pathways and major points in order to better utilize the energies in the body. The Eight Treasures adjusts the spine with all energy channels in the body. We will also discuss the relationship between the Eight Treasures and the eight extraordinary channels, their functions, and how they are activated for the purpose of cultivation.

4
The Channels and Points

The human body is a microcosm of the universe. Like a miniature universe, the cyclical and constant movement and transformation of fluids, molecules, cells, chemicals and energies within the body characterize life. As water springs forth from the deep earth and flows into streams and then rivers and finally the sea, the *chi* or life force traverses the body within tributaries and canals that we call channels. The 12 main channels each correspond to a particular organ. And not unlike the self-sustaining universe, the *chi* flows perpetually, filling the empty and draining the excess from parts of the body regulated by an intrinsic balancing mechanism. Therefore, the channels play an important role in the healthy functioning of human life.

There are eight extraordinary channels. These eight channels are called "extraordinary" because of their unique function and pathways. They function as reservoirs to store and release *chi* depending on the state of the 12 main channels. The most important of the eight extraordinary channels are the Governing (*Du*) and the Conception (*Ren*) channels that run along the midline in the back and front of the body respectively. The pathways of the 12 main channels are described below.

The Twelve Main Channels

The organ systems use the channels as an invisible network of communication. They are not based on a nerve, vessel, or lymphatic circulation path. The channels are distinct and specific pathways through which *chi* and messages/information are transported. The channels run symmetrically along both sides of the body.

The accompanying illustrations show the pathways and points that rise to the surface of the body. Note that the channels also have internal pathways, which are too complex to discuss here.

These are the approximate pathways of the channels:

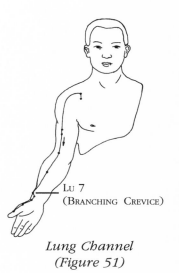

Lu 7
(Branching Crevice)

Lung Channel
(Figure 51)

1. Lung Channel (Abbreviated: Lu)

Starts at the front of the shoulder and runs down the inside of the arm to the end of the thumb.

2. Large Intestine Channel (LI)

Starts from the end of the index finger and runs up the outside of the arm, to the top of the shoulder, up the side of the neck and crosses over the upper lip to the opposite side just along the side of the nostril.

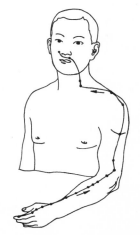

Large Intestine Channel
(Figure 52)

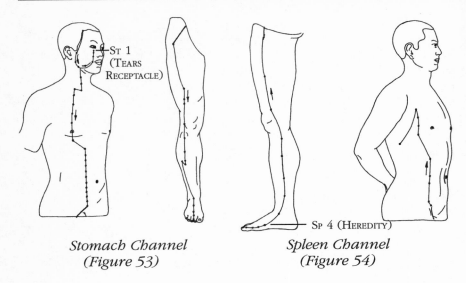

Stomach Channel
(Figure 53)

Spleen Channel
(Figure 54)

3. Stomach Channel (St)

Starts just below the eye, runs down the cheek, down the front side of the neck, down the chest through the nipple, stomach, abdomen, front of the thigh, knee, shin and to the lateral end of the second toe.

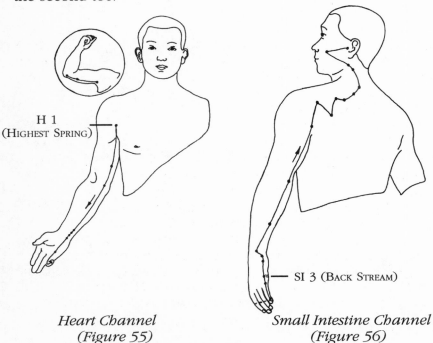

Heart Channel
(Figure 55)

Small Intestine Channel
(Figure 56)

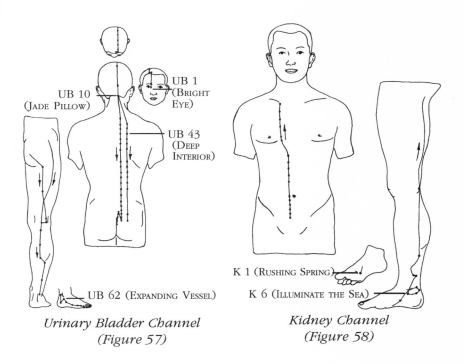

Urinary Bladder Channel
(Figure 57)

Kidney Channel
(Figure 58)

4. Spleen Channel (Sp)
Starts from the medial side of the big toe, up the inside of the ankle, up the inside of the lower leg, knee, thigh, lower abdomen, and up to the side of the rib cage.

5. Heart Channel (H)
Starts in the armpit and runs down the inner side of the arm to the end of the little finger.

6. Small Intestine Channel (SI)
From the little finger, it runs up the back side of the arm, criss-crosses through the shoulder blades, up the side of the neck and the side of the face, to the front of the ear.

7. Bladder (Urinary Bladder) Channel (UB)
Starts at the inside corner of the eye, runs up the corner of the eyebrow straight over the head, down to the base of the skull, the base of the neck, down along the band of muscles along the spine

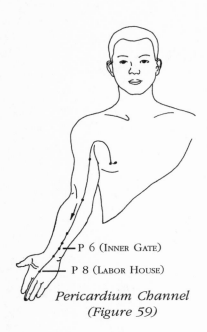

P 6 (INNER GATE)

P 8 (LABOR HOUSE)

Pericardium Channel
(Figure 59)

to the buttock, down the back of the thigh, the back of the knee, the back of the calf, to the outside of the ankle and of the foot, and ends at the outside of the small toe.

8. Kidney Channel (K)

Starts from K 1 (Rushing Spring) point in the center of the sole of the foot, runs up the inside of the foot to the inside of the ankle, up the inside of the leg, the knee, the lower back, through the body to the lower abdomen, up alongside the navel (belly button), alongside the center of the chest and ends at the collarbone.

9. Pericardium Channel (P)

Starts near the outside of the nipple, runs down the inside middle of the arm down to the end of the middle finger.

10. Triple Warmer or Triple Heater "*San Jiao*" Channel (SJ)

Starts from the ring finger on the side next to the small finger, runs up along the outside center of the arm, up the shoulder to the ear, around the back of the ear and to the outside of the eyebrow.

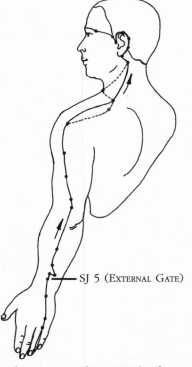

SJ 5 (EXTERNAL GATE)

Triple Warmer (San Jiao) Channel
(Figure 60)

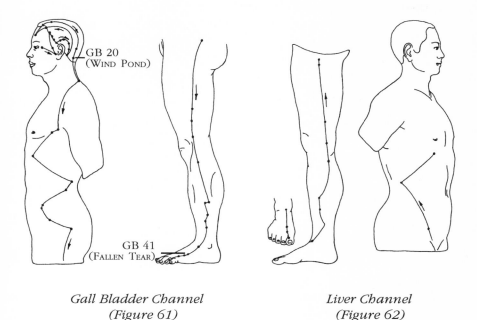

Gall Bladder Channel
(Figure 61)

Liver Channel
(Figure 62)

11. Gall Bladder Channel (GB)

Starts from the outside of the eye socket, runs in front of the ear, up the side of the head, up and down in an arc on the side of the head, and comes down to the shoulder, down the side of the body to the front of the armpit, zigzags across the rib cage and the side of the abdomen and buttock, down the outside center of the thigh and calf, and down to between the small toe and fourth toe on each foot.

12. Liver Channel (L)

Starts from between the big toe and second toe on the foot, runs up the inside of the ankle, leg and thigh, through the genitals and up to the liver in the lower chest.

As each of the channels follows its specific course of circulation, the free flow and sufficiency of *chi* (vital energy), or their opposites – blockage or insufficiency – are bound to be manifested at the area supplied by the channel. The twelve main channels connect with and pertain to the organs, and disorders of the organs will be reflected in the corresponding channels. It is possible, therefore, to determine which channel is affected by studying the location and characteristics of the symptoms and signs.

The main pathological manifestations of the twelve regular channels may be described as follows:

1. The Lung Channel: Cough, asthma, hemoptysis, congested and sore throat, sensation of fullness in chest, pain in the supraclavicular fossa, shoulder, back and the anterior border of the medial aspect of the arm.

2. The Large Intestine Channel: Epistaxis, watery nasal discharge, toothache, congested and sore throat, pain in the neck, anterior part of the shoulder and anterior border of the extension aspect of the upper limb, borborygmus, abdominal pain, diarrhea, constipation, dysentery.

3. The Stomach Channel: Borborygmus, abdominal distension, edema, epigastric pain, vomiting, feeling of hunger, epistaxis, deviation of eyes and mouth, congested and sore throat, pain in the chest, abdomen and lateral aspect of the lower limbs, fever, mental disturbance.

4. The Spleen Channel: Belching, vomiting, epigastric pain, abdominal distension, loose stools, jaundice, sluggishness and general malaise, stiffness and pain at the root of the tongue, swelling and coldness in the medial aspect of the thigh and knee.

5. The Heart Channel: Cardialgia, palpitation, hypochondriac pain, insomnia, night sweating, dryness of the throat, thirst, pain in the medial aspect of the upper arm, feverishness in palms.

6. The Small Intestine Channel: Deafness, yellow sclera, sore throat, swelling of the cheek, distension and pain in the lower abdomen, frequent urination, pain along the posterior border of the lateral aspect of the shoulder and arm.

7. The Bladder (Urinary Bladder) Channel: Retention of urine, enuresis, mental disturbance, malaria, ophthalmodynia, lacrimation when exposed to wind, nasal obstruction, rhinitis, epistaxis, headache, pain in the nape, upper and lower back, buttocks and posterior aspect of lower limbs.

8. The Kidney Channel: Enuresis, frequent urination, nocturnal emission, impotence, irregular menstruation, asthma, hemoptysis, dryness of the tongue, congested and sore throat, edema, lumbago, pain along the spinal column and the medial aspect of the thigh, weakness of the lower limbs, feverish sensation in soles.

9. The Pericardium Channel: Cardialgia, palpitation, mental restlessness, stifling feeling in chest, flushed face, swelling in the axilla, mental disturbance, spasm of the upper limbs, feverishness in palms.

10. The Triple Warmer (*San Jiao*) Channel: Abdominal distension, edema, enuresis, dysuria, deafness, tinnitus, pain in the outer canthus, swelling of the cheeks, congested and sore throat, pain in the retroauricular region, shoulder, and lateral aspect of the arm and elbow.

11. The Gall Bladder Channel: Headache, pain in the outer canthus, pain in the jaw, blurring of vision, bitter taste in mouth, swelling and pain in the supraclavicular fossa, pain in the axilla, pain along the lateral aspect of the chest, hypochondrium, thigh and lower limbs.

12. The Liver Channel: Low back pain, fullness in the chest, pain in the lower abdomen, hernia, vertical headache, dryness of the throat, hiccup, enuresis, dysuria, mental disturbance.

The Eight Extraordinary Channels
The eight extraordinary channels may be viewed as a regulating mechanism or reservoir for the twelve channels. When there is an excess or deficiency of energy (post-natal *chi*) along the twelve main channels, the eight extraordinary channels start to function. They store excess energy (post-natal *chi*) or provide energy (prenatal *chi*) from the kidney organ system. This "give and take" reservoir process is a self-regulating function but can be activated and accessed through control points. These control points may be viewed as points where energy converges. You can also regard them as automatic valves, so when you practice the Eight Treasures you don't have to wonder whether you need to store or draw upon energy. The storing or providing function will happen automatically as you practice.

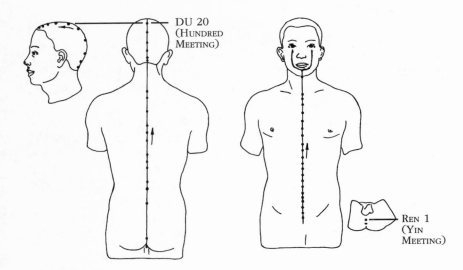

Governing (Du) Channel
(Figure 63)

Conception (Ren) Channel
(Figure 64)

The eight extraordinary channels have their own distinct pathways. They borrow points by crisscrossing the 12 main channels, except for the Governing *(Du)* and Conception *(Ren)*, which have their own distinct points.

The pathways of the eight extraordinary channels are described as follows.

1. The Governing (*Du*) Channel
Originates from the inside of the lower abdomen. Descending, it emerges at the perineum and then ascends along the interior of the spinal column to the nape, where it enters the brain, ascends to the vertex, and comes down the forehead to below the nose.

2. The Conception (*Ren*) Channel
Originates from the lower abdomen and emerges from the perineum. It runs to the pubic region and ascends up the front midline to the throat. Running further upward, it curves around the lips,

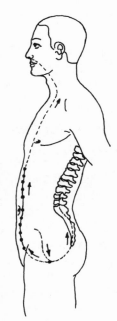

Vitality
(Chong Mai) Channel
(Figure 65)

passes through the cheek and enters the region below the eyes.

3. The Vitality *(Chong Mai)* Channel

Originates in the lower abdomen, descends and emerges from the perineum. It then ascends and runs inside the vertebral column, while its superficial portion passes above the genitals where it splits into two and coincides with the Kidney channel, running up to the throat and curving around the lips.

4. The Belt *(Dai Mai)* Channel

Starts below the hypochondriac region (below the lowest rib). Running obliquely downward, it runs transversely around the waist like a belt.

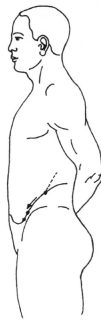

Belt (Dai Mai) Channel (Figure 66)

5. The *Yang* Connecting *(Yang Qiao)* Channel

Starts from the lateral side of the heel. Ascending along the leg, it goes along the lateral aspect of the thigh. From there, it winds over to the shoulder and ascends along the neck to the corner of the mouth. Then it enters the inner corner of the eye to communicate with the *Yin* Connecting *(Yin Qiao)* channel. It then runs further upward along the Urinary Bladder channel to the forehead where it meets the Gall Bladder channel.

6. The *Yin* Connecting *(Yin Qiao)* Channel

Starts on the inside of the foot in front of the ankle bone and ascends, running upward along the leg and thigh to the external genitalia. From there it ascends up the chest to the collarbone.

Yang Connecting (Yang Qiao) Channel (Figure 67)

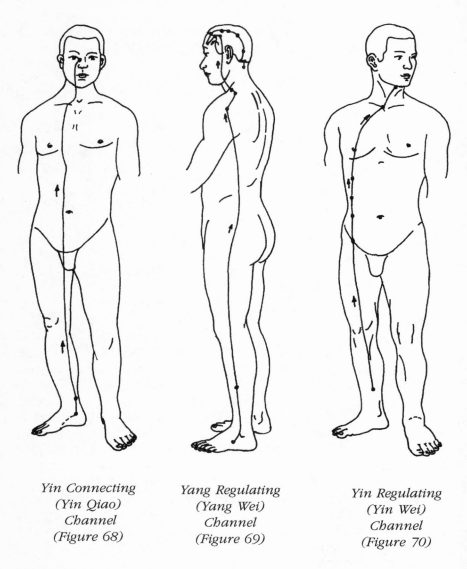

Yin Connecting
(Yin Qiao)
Channel
(Figure 68)

Yang Regulating
(Yang Wei)
Channel
(Figure 69)

Yin Regulating
(Yin Wei)
Channel
(Figure 70)

Running further upward alongside the Adam's apple and then along the cheekbone, it reaches the inner corner of the eye and communicates with the *Yang* Connecting *(Yang Qiao)* channel.

7. The *Yang* Regulating *(Yang Wei)* Channel

Begins at the side of the foot. Ascending to the external ankle bone, it runs upward along the Gall Bladder channel, passing through the hip region and further upward to below the ribs and rib region and the posterior armpit to the shoulder. From there it further ascends to the forehead and then turns backward to the back of the neck, where it communicates with the Governing (*Du*) channel.

8. The *Yin* Regulating (*Yin Wei*) Channel
Starts from the inside of the leg and ascends along the thigh to the abdomen to communicate with the Spleen channel. Then it runs along the chest and communicates with the Conception (*Ren*) channel at the neck.

The Eight Control Points
Eight energy points called control or confluent points are used to activate the eight extraordinary channels at locations where they communicate with the 12 main channels. These points are stimulated or focused upon during various times in the practice of the Eight Treasures. Their locations are described below (the control points are illustrated on the figures showing the channels):

SI 3 (Back Stream point) activates the Governing (*Du*) channel: When a loose fist is made, the point is in the depression at the end of the crease below the base of the little finger. See Figure 56.

Lu 7 (Branching Crevice point) activates the Conception (*Ren*) channel: On the side of the forearm just above the bony prominence, about one and a half thumb widths above the inside crease of the wrist at the base of the thumb. See Figure 51.

Sp 4 (Heredity point) activates the Vitality (*Chong Mai*) channel: On the inside of the foot, above the middle arch, in the depression below and in front of the bone extending back from the big toe. See Figure 54.

GB 41 (Fallen Tear point) activates the Belt (*Dai Mai*) channel: About one inch toward the ankle from the junction of the two smallest toes (in the depression behind the small tendon and between the bones). See Figure 61.

UB 62 (Expanding Vessel point) activates the *Yang* Connecting (*Yang Qiao*) channel: In the depression directly below the tip of the ankle bone on the outside of the leg (opposite K 6 (Illuminate the Sea). See Figure 57.

K 6 (Illuminate the Sea point) activates the *Yin* Connecting (*Yin Qiao*) channel: Opposite UB 62 (Expanding Vessel). In the depression directly below the inner tip of the ankle bone. See Figure 58.

SJ 5 (External Gate point) activates the *Yang* Regulating (*Yang Wei*) Channel: Two thumb widths away from the crease of the wrist on the outside forearm, halfway between the bones, opposite P 6 (Inner Gate). See Figure 60.

P 6 (Inner Gate point) activates the *Yin* Regulating (*Yin Wei*) channel: Opposite SJ 5 (External Gate point), two thumb widths away from the crease of the wrist on the inside forearm (between the two tendons). See Figure 59.

When there is an overabundance of post-natal *chi* in the twelve channels, stimulating these points causes the excess *chi* to be channeled off and stored in the kidneys. When the twelve channels are depleted, stimulation of these points activates withdrawal of the saved or stored energy. This is the same concept as a bank account, with ideally only deposits and no withdrawals!

Also, UB 1 (Bright Eye point, see Figure 57) located at the inside corner of the eyes, is a very important point used in acupuncture as well as for cultivation. This point is very close to the pituitary gland, the master gland. It is responsible for stimulating hormonal functions. This point is activated by the "staring" action in some of the Eight Treasures. For example, whenever you turn your head to the left, if you roll the eyes toward the upper left corner of the eye sockets and stare, it will be activated.

It is said that when you practice the Eight Treasures, all *chi* ascends to *Du* 20 (Hundred Meeting point or *Bai Hui*, see Figure 63), which is the point on the very top of the head, and then all the energy ascends from the head at that point. That is the ultimate achievement which few people experience. It takes time to accomplish successful cultivation. To do so, the pure *yang* energy (which is symbolic of your spirit in this instance) rises or ascends to the invisible opening at *Du* 20 (Hundred Meeting point) on the top of the head and out; this is where the achieved spirit would leave the body at the right time. This also explains why in the

Eight Treasures and other *t'ai chi* movements there is a lot of lifting the *chi* up to Du 20 (Hundred Meeting Point).

The objective of health is to cultivate and maintain the unceasing balanced flow of *chi* in the 12 main channels so that the essential functions of the body remain optimal. The objective of spiritual development is to gather, cultivate and refine the *chi* within the eight extraordinary channels so that the pre-natal *chi* can be transformed to assist the *shen* or the spirit.

The Eight Treasures and other internal arts are an individualized effort to maintain the balance of your *chi*. The science and art of acupuncture can quickly and precisely accomplish the manipulation of *chi* flow in the body.

Path of *Chi* Circulation

The following is the typical path of *chi* circulation. The stomach and spleen system produces nutritive *chi* by extracting the essence of food. From the middle warmer (middle *jiao*, in which the stomach/spleen have absorbed nutritive *chi*), post-natal *chi* is then transported to the Lung channel in the upper cavity. The energy transportation/circulation cycle starts with the Lung channel.

Channel	*yin* or *yang*	Peak Time
1. Lung	*yin*	3 - 5 a.m.
2. Large Intestine	*yang*	5 - 7 a.m.
3. Stomach	*yang*	7 - 9 a.m.
4. Spleen	*yin*	9 - 11 a.m.
5. Heart	*yin*	11 - 1 p.m.
6. Small Intestine	*yang*	1 - 3 p.m.
7. U. Bladder	*yang*	3 - 5 p.m.
8. Kidney	*yin*	5 - 7 p.m.
9. Pericardium	*yin*	7 - 9 p.m.
10. Triple Warmer	*yang*	9 - 11 p.m.
11. Gall Bladder	*yang*	11 - 1 a.m.
12. Liver	*yin*	1 - 3 a.m.

This is according to the solar clock (which is not affected by daylight-saving time).

The energy flow is a natural cycle that takes 24 hours to complete. The Eight Treasures, however, promotes total circulation during the 45 minutes or one hour that it takes to practice it. Thus, you can make one complete energy cycle while performing the Eight Treasures instead of waiting 24 hours for this to happen by itself. It is helpful to circulate your energy more frequently to rejuvenate and nourish your body.

The Two Primary Channels

The Governing (*Du*) and Conception (*Ren*) channels are the two primary extraordinary channels. The Governing (*Du*) channel is the *yang* part of the energy cycle. The Conception (*Ren*) channel is the *yin* part of the energy cycle.

The energy or *chi* in the Governing (*Du*) channel circulates from 6:01 a.m. to 6:00 p.m., a 12-hour period, representing the *yang*, active phase of a human life. The energy or *chi* in the Conception (*Ren*) channel circulates from 6:01 p.m. to 6:00 a.m., the other twelve hours, representing the *yin* phase.

Microcosmic and Macrocosmic Orbits

Within the energy circulation systems, there are two main circulatory orbits. These orbits are analogous to the stars whose orbits are synchronized to ensure their survival.

The microcosmic orbit uses the Governing (*Du*) and Conception (*Ren*) channels. The macrocosmic orbit consists of the twelve channels and the eight extraordinary channels. Thus, the macrocosmic orbit also includes the Governing (*Du*) and Conception (*Ren*) channels.

The microcosmic orbit, more specifically, follows the Governing (*Du*) channel from the kidneys to the perineum, up the spine, over the head, down the front of the face to the roof of the mouth, goes down the inside of the body through the trunk and into the kidneys and then picks up where the Conception (*Ren*) channel starts, which is from the kidneys, emerges at the perineum and goes up the front of the body, to the bottom of the tongue and then down the inside of the body to connect with the Governing (*Du*) channel.

The macrocosmic orbit involves *chi* circulation in all 14 channels, that is, the 12 basic channels plus the Governing (*Du*) and Conception (*Ren*) channels. Before you engage in any special practice that follows the macrocosmic orbit, you should learn from an experienced teacher. It is safer and more beneficial to practice the Eight Treasures in order to achieve such circulation. As described previously, the Eight Treasures circulates *chi* throughout the channels in a sequence and system that supports your overall health, well-being and self-development.

Microcosmic Orbit   **Macrocosmic Orbit**

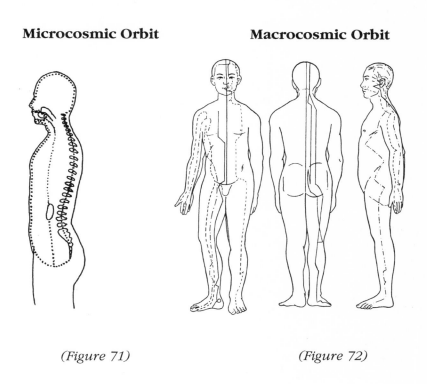

(Figure 71)   (Figure 72)

V
Self-Cultivation

Let us revisit the two aspects of cultivation: the external aspect of virtuous fulfillment in your life, which involves your fellow men and women; and the internal aspect of practicing methods and techniques for self-improvement. Each life is self-responsible, and in self-cultivation each person takes responsibility for his or her own health (physical, mental and spiritual). Both aspects of cultivation are very important, and neither can be neglected.

The Importance of Virtue in Cultivation

In energy cultivation, it is very important that you place equal emphasis on the development of virtue along with your practices, because the process of building is very slow but the process of destruction is very fast. A serious cultivator will ingrain this principle in his or her heart and never stray from the path!

A person can throw away twenty years of cultivation in one day. An example of a destructive element to your cultivation can be intense anger or a deviation from a simple, natural lifestyle that may cause you to become distracted and discontinue daily cultivation. For example, a person who has diligently meditated and been virtuous for twenty years can one day in meditation have a thought like, "I now have certain powers and abilities and can use them to exploit other people." Just having one thought like that can totally change a person's energy. It contaminates all aspects of your *chi*, and since your *chi* is now the manifestation of your being, your energy and behavior will now contain the message of this negative information. The next thing that might happen is a tangible action, just because of this one thought, and that would destroy all the years of cultivation. This is why the ancients advised to keep straight on the path!

This may seem like an extreme example. However, do not consider anything to be negligible, because *any* negative influence is eventually detrimental. Any step off the path is dangerous. You must regard it as seriously as that!

Stay on the Right Path

The ancient developed ones were known to be extremely secretive. Why do you suppose that was? Was it because they were selfish and did not wish to share with the world? No, the natural principles of spiritual development are ultimately in alignment with the eternity of life, and one of the virtues of universal life is to be of service to humankind. So how was it that they kept their secrets from people, yet claimed to be of service to humankind?

Their reasons were practical ones. Can you imagine the consequences if people who were not well disciplined and did not have control over themselves became well versed in the science of internal alchemy? They could damage themselves and cause trouble for others. The damage could be physical, mental, or spiritual, and the consequences could be significant. Thus, responsible masters are careful about sharing their secrets.

I will give you just one example. There have been many searchers of spirituality in the West who have gone to other countries to explore various spiritual traditions. I do not want to single out any tradition, but only mention this because I have had direct experience with patients who pursued certain practices in order to reach spiritual enlightenment. In the end, some of them became insane and unable to cope with normal life. They separate themselves from the world; some commit suicide and others end up in mental institutions.

When you come to a juncture in your development and in your practice where you possess certain knowledge, if you are not ready to be at that stage, and you are not truly prepared to go further but you still venture forth, disasters can happen.

Some students have an admirable quality of being sincere and dedicated. However, their mistake is that they want more than they are ready for. This is where their serious trouble lies.

Balanced Development
Responsible masters are concerned with balanced development. Simply changing your physical destiny to live longer is not enough; you must also mature psychologically and spiritually. If you live to be 120 years old and have the mind of a 12-year old, with the same negative emotional patterns, what good does that do you or those around you? The approach of the Integral Way of Life is to cultivate and refine oneself naturally, not artificially. By refining the mind, body, and spirit through various practices, the developed ones were able to change their genetic destiny.

Obviously, intellectualizing or only thinking about this material will not help you experience the natural flow of *chi*. Only those who diligently practice the Eight Treasures and other internal arts experience *chi* as it travels smoothly and activates the channels. The purpose of the previous material is to help you recognize where the sensations occur in different parts of your body or energy channels and be able to move the *chi* with your mind by first visualizing the pathways. Guiding the *chi* with the mind is an important aspect of *chi gong*.

In time, you will actually feel physical sensations such as fluttering near certain points or itching like a bug crawling along the channel, a warm flow of liquid, tingling, expansion, etc. People have different experiences, but whatever you experience, do not become fascinated or excited. Just continue to practice and do not become distracted by the experiences or by your thoughts. Continue your visualization, and gradually you will develop the power to move the *chi*. It is not a placebo effect to feel energy. Energy is a definite reality in the body, even though it may not be readily seen. Do the movements correctly, and learn about what areas of the body and what channels each one affects. The Eight Treasures are an invaluable tool for taking care of yourself.

6
Understanding Deepens Your Practice

As you practice the Eight Treasures over the years, your experience will change. Your interest and energy manifestations are also different. The following information about each of the Treasures and movements can help increase your understanding and deepen your practice.

Warm-Up

The Warm-Up is very important to do prior to the start of the Eight Treasures because it activates the flow of *chi* in all parts of the body. The Warm-Up is also good for relieving stress.

The basic Warm-Up movements are described in Chapter 3, Learning the Movements of the Eight Treasures. You can now learn more about them.

Basic Warm-Up Movements

Tapping the Trunk

Use the loose fist and gentle tapping to stimulate the *chi*. Start tapping two inches below the navel, following the midline up to the navel, then moving from the navel to the sides of the chest and to the top of the shoulders.

Tapping the Trunk and Arms

Using the right hand, start tapping from the side of the trunk just below the armpit, following the *Yin* Regulating *(Yin Wei)* channel (the spleen and gall bladder area.) This area is almost never exercised or stimulated and there are a lot of vital organs in this area. (There are also lymph nodes in the armpit area which benefit from this stimulation.) Move down the left side, and then starting from the front of the pelvic area, move upward in a straight line to just before the shoulders. Then, with the left arm extended palm up, continue tapping on the inside of the arm near the armpit and down to the wrist. Turn the arm over and continue tapping along the other side of the wrist, and move up along the arm to the shoulder area. Continue this gentle tapping up and around the shoulder area. You can do this longer until you feel warmth in your hands and when it feels that the body is warming up. Repeat this on the other side.

Tapping the Back and Legs
With both hands, you should be tapping on the Kidney points or lower back area. This is very beneficial for the adrenal glands. Then come down the side of the thighs, legs and ankles. This is beneficial for the Urinary Bladder and Gall Bladder channels.

Come up the insides of the ankles, legs, thighs and near the crotch area with the same tapping. At the crotch area (where again there are lymph nodes which benefit), alternate bending and straightening both knees as you tap to loosen up congestion in this area. This tapping further facilitates the opening of the Belt (*Dai Mai*) channel.

> Advanced Students: If your intent is to activate the smooth flow of *chi*, the direction of the tapping should follow the same direction the *chi* flows.
>
> Stimulating in the reverse direction is done to push the *chi*, to create a resistance or accumulation. This builds up *chi* that is trying to push the other way, causing tremendous resistance. The effect is a stimulation.

Swinging the Arms Back and Jumping Up
Swing both arms backward and raise ankles in synchrony. With repetition, the swinging can be more vigorous and the ankles can raise higher to jump up with the swing. End this movement by winding down to its initial intensity. This works the shoulder and armpit, activating the heart which houses the spirit. The shoulder swinging helps awaken your *shen* (refined *chi* or spirit) to help you stay alert.

Additional Warm-Up Movements

• After raising the arms while tapping along the front and arm channels, do a big shoulder rotation by stepping with the right foot at 45 degrees and pulling the right shoulder up and down in a circle. The right arm can just hang straight down and the left hand can be near the *tan tien* or also just let it hang down. Repeat on the opposite side for the left shoulder.

• Do a small shoulder rotation, forward and backward. This is done without moving any other part of the torso, just the shoulders.

• Shake wrists to loosen them up.

• Last but not least, "shake your *tan tien*." With feet shoulder-width apart, your spine and sphincter muscles tight, hands hanging loosely on the sides, start a gentle shaking from your *tan tien*. This shaking should shake and stimulate (slightly) the *tan tien/* pelvis. Do this for about five minutes. This gentle vibratory action will move the energy to every part of the body. Some days you will shake like the wind and sometimes you will shake in a nice gentle fashion. Your body will naturally tell you what to do. Your movement also depends on your physiological state. This movement stimulates many parts of the body, but most importantly it stimulates the endocrine system. The mild stimulation of the reproductive organs activates the hormones. It is a very good movement, so do not skip this in the warm-up.

> Advanced Students: You have activated/stimulated the *chi* flow during this warm-up and you will not hurt yourself. Daily activation of the *chi* flow is very beneficial. All this is designed to free up potential blockages.

First Treasure
Sustaining Heaven with Both Hands
to Adjust the Three Warmers

The First Treasure works on nourishing the physical body. The main purpose of the five movements is to move your energy upward. You can easily observe that when people are weak, their muscle systems drop down. Have you seen the muscles drop down in people's faces? That means they are worn out and old. Also, the stomach drops down, or in a weak woman, the uterus drops down.

The ancient achieved ones knew that it is very important to unite the physical body with the mind. They said, "The root of a tree is at the bottom, and does not move; but the root of people is at the top, thus they are free in action and movement." Therefore, the First Treasure prevents the muscles from dropping down by moving the energy up.

The first movement of the First Treasure relieves nervous tension and tightness. You utilize the movement to relax your muscles such as in the shoulders and waist; open all joints, and also stretch the joints of the knees and ankles. By doing that, you relax or untie your whole body system; then your movement can reach from the tip of your toes to the tip of the fingers and hair. In the first section, although there is some bending movement up and down, the main goal is to make your body respond inwardly from outward movement.

Action: Strengthens and balances the respiratory, endocrine, digestive, and elimination systems.

• increases blood and energy in the thoracic and abdominal cavities
• balances the triple warmer
• corrects bad posture in the upper back and chest
• expands lung capacity, increases oxygen intake, and rids the body of carbon dioxide
• relieves frozen shoulder and bursitis of the upper extremities
• removes fatigue
• mixes energy of Heaven and Earth

1.A. Move the Stars and Turn the Big Dipper:
This first movement of the Eight Treasures begins by mobilizing the major *yin* storage in the body, namely from the *Yin* Connecting *(Yin Qiao)* and Conception *(Ren)* channels and the Kidney channel.

• gathers *chi* from Heaven
• brings heavenly *chi* through the trunk
• communicates and integrates the energies of Earth, Human and Heaven
• mixes the *chi* of the viscera

• gathers *chi* from earth
• activates K 6 (Illuminate the Sea point) on the inside of the ankle and the *Yin* Conducting (*Yin Qiao*) channel
• brings *chi* through the Conception (*Ren*) channel and out at the top of the head at *Du* 20 (Hundred Meeting Point, *Bai Hui*)
• the beak hand grasps the *chi* with its motion
• stimulates the Lu 7 (Branching Crevice) control point by bending and stretching the wrist

Move the Stars

> Advanced Students: Connect the heavenly energy to *Du* 20 (Hundred Meeting Point) and guide the energy down the Kidney channel to the crotch area. This movement also harvests energy from the three *Jiao* (warmers) - upper, middle and lower.

•Extraordinary Channel: Upper portion of *Yin* Regulating *(Yin Wei)*.
•Other Points: Kidney channel, *Du* 20 (Hundred Meeting Point*).
Comment: Refinement means being able to gather *chi* from the twelve channels and from the environment (the earth, trees, air, moon, stars and sun). Humans are already endowed with the higher qualities of spirit and consciousness. As you become achieved, you will learn how to extract energy from nature. Some people who do not refine their spirit block or muddle it and remain no more refined than animals.

Turn the Big Dipper

> Advanced Students: Bring up the energy from K 6 (Illuminate the Sea) to UB 1 (Bright Eye) and Lu 7 (Branching Crevice). Visualize this path; use your bright eye energy to look at your wrist, and energy will converge on Lu 7 (Branching Crevice). K 6 (Illuminate the Sea) and Lu 7 (Branching Crevice) connect the upper and lower points of the body's major *yin* channels.

•Extraordinary Channels: Major *yin* channels - *Yin* Connecting *(Yin Qiao)* and Conception *(Ren)*
•Control Points: K 6 (Illuminate the Sea), UB 1 (Bright Eye) and Lu 7 (Branching Crevice)
•Comment: This is a *yin* movement. In the interplay between *yin* and *yang* energies, the *yin* and *yang* always move separately. *Yin* and *yang* movements alternate but never mix. The beak at the base of the spine closes the *yang* channel. The *yang* energy is not activated in this movement, but balances the movement through its quiet stability (having a strong back).

1.B. The Great Elephant Raises Its Trunk:
• activates *chi* flow in the Belt (*Dai Mai*) channel
• gathers *chi* from earth, touch GB 41 (Fallen Tear) on feet
• brings *chi* through Conception (*Ren*) channel in mid-trunk
• raises *chi* to top of head and out at *Du* 20 (Hundred Meeting Point)

> Advanced Students: As you raise your hands, you connect them to the Governing (*Du*) channel and to *Du* 20 (Hundred Meeting point).

•Extraordinary Channels: Belt (*Dai Mai*) and Conception (*Ren*) connect to the Governing (*Du*)
•Control Points: GB 41 (Fallen Tear) and Lu 7 (Branching Crevice)
•Comment: This movement brings energy from earth through the body to connect with heavenly energy at *Du* 20 (Hundred Meeting Point) Further, this energy integrates all channels through the Belt (*Dai Mai*) channel.

1.C. The Dolphin's Fins Pat the Water:
• activates GB 41 (Fallen Tear) and the Liver channel
• draws *chi* from the Liver channel along the insides of the legs up to the groin/sexual glands
• brings *chi* to the Belt (*Dai Mai*) channel
• compresses *chi* into *lower tan tien*

> Advanced Students: The organs that are affected are the gall bladder and liver. This movement can release a blockage or provide a gentle massage.

- **Extraordinary Channel**: Belt *(Dai Mai)*
- **Control Point**: GB 41 (Fallen Tear)
- **Comment**: This movement opens up or helps clear blockages in the reproductive and genital areas. It also sedates the liver to calm anger. The Belt *(Dai Mai)* channel pulls everything together to tonify and invigorate the flow of *chi*.

1.D. Bringing the Sea to the Top of the Mountain:

The actions of this movement include expanding the three warmers. Look straight up during the backbend at the beginning (this stimulates the Governing or *Du* channel).

When the hands are clasped behind the head, keep them clasped with thumbs pressing on the UB 10 (Jade Pillow) point. When the hands are clasped behind the head, and also later as the arms stretch over the head, stimulate SI 3 (Back Stream) of each hand by touching it with the tip of the little finger of the other hand.

When you twist and look up, the stretch is felt at the sides and kidney area. When you sit and crouch, touch the elbows to K 6 (Illuminate the Sea) inside each ankle to activate *the Yin* Connecting *(Yin Qiao)* channel.

Rise and push *chi* up and out *Du* 20 (Hundred Meeting Point) at the top of the head.

> Advanced Students: Visualize the *Yang* Connecting *(Yang Qiao)* and the *Yin* Connecting *(Yin Qiao)* coming up as hands extend out. When you rise from the crouched position, visualize the path from UB 62 (Expanding Vessel) and K 6 (Illuminate the Sea) to the forehead and to *Du* 20 (Hundred Meeting Point) as you stretch up and out to the sides.

- **Extraordinary Channels**: *Yang* Connecting *(Yang Qiao)*, *Yin* Connecting *(Yin Qiao)*, Governing *(Du)*

•Control Points: UB 62 (Expanding Vessel), K 6 (Illuminate the Sea), SI 3 (Back Stream)
•Comment: Bring the energy flow from K 6 (Illuminate the Sea which is also called Reflecting Sea) to the top of the head at *Du* 20 (Hundred Meeting Point also called "The Vertex" or "The Top").

1.E. Water and Fire Meet:

Touch the high point of the arch and inside ankle as you come up. (Note: the Kidney channel runs through the inner arch and ankle arc.) The backs of the hands should be touching as they come up to open the chest area. The fingers should be like open claws.

• stimulates Sp 4 (Heredity) in the inside of the feet and activates the Vitality (*Chong Mai*) channel
• brings *yin chi* up the legs, through the groin and into the chest cavity
• *yin* or water *chi* mixes with heart or fire *chi* in the chest
• bending hands back at the end stimulates P 6 (Inner Gate) and activates the *Yin* Regulating (*Yin Wei*) channel
• push *chi* out at P 8 (Labor House) in the palm

> Advanced Students: Water represents the kidneys and fire represents the heart fire in the chest. Water energy is raised to the chest and mixed with fire energy in an alchemical process which results in "steam" or *chi*. The steam is brought to the control point by pushing out the hands with the mind focused on P 6 (Inner Gate) and P 8 (Labor House).

•Extraordinary Channels: Vitality (*Chong Mai*), *Yin* Connecting (*Yin Qiao*), *Yin* Regulating (*Yin Wei*) and Conception (*Ren*). *Yin* Connecting (*Yin Qiao*) is activated as you come up. Vitality (*Chong Mai*) and Conception (*Ren*) are activated as your hands come up and open the chest area. *Yin* Regulating (*Yin Wei*) is stimulated by the shoulder motion in the front. Focus on P 6 (Inner Gate) for this movement.
•Control Points: Sp 4 (Heredity), K 6 (Illuminate the Sea), P 6 (Inner Gate), Lu 7 (Branching Crevice).
•Comment: This movement also activates the thymus gland.

Second Treasure:
Drawing the Bow with Both Hands to Aim at a Distant Target

The movements of the Second Treasure conduct your energy horizontally by stretching both sides to different directions like up and down, left and right, etc. The trunk of your body mainly contains three sections, and the five movements in the Second Treasure guide your energy to the center section by moving both sides symmetrically. This brings balanced development.

Action: Strengthens and balances the cerebral-spinal, tendo-muscular, and immune systems.
• benefits the upper warmer
• enhances respiration and blood circulation
• strengthens thoracic and intercostal muscles
• reduces lactic acid build up
• dilates the coronary arteries
• prevents sagging breasts
• increases respiratory capacity

2.A. The Great Bird Spreads Its Wings:
This movement encourages exhalation and opens the chest cavity/upper warmer.
• stimulate P 6 (Inner Gate) by bending the wrist and activating the *Yin* Regulating (*Yin Wei*) channel
• exhale *chi* out P 8 (Labor House) in the palms

> Advanced Students: Gather *chi* and bring it up to the chest. Concentrate on P 6 (Inner Gate) when hands are stretched out.

•Extraordinary Channels: *Yin* Regulating *(Yin Wei)* and *Yang* Connecting *(Yang Qiao)*. *Yin* Regulating *(Yin Wei)* is stimulated at the chest area and *Yang* Connecting *(Yang Qiao)* by the horse stance. Governing *(Du)* is stimulated by the mild bouncing.
•Control Points: P 6 (Inner Gate), UB 62 (Expanding Vessel), SI 3 (Back Stream)
•Comment: This is a continuation of the last movement in the First Treasure, which promotes and refines the flow of fire/steam in the heart and stomach areas.

2.B. Drawing the Bow:
• gathers *chi* in the upper warmer
• touch SI 3 (Back Stream) of the aiming hand with the index finger of the other *during the gather*, to activate the Governing *(Du)* channel
• keep the spine straight and neck turned to stimulate flow in the Governing *(Du)* channel
• flexing of index finger stimulates the Large Intestine channel

> Advanced Students: This movement is also good for constipation because it stimulates the large intestine.

•Extraordinary Channels: *Yang* Connecting *(Yang Qiao)*
•Control Points: UB 62 (Expanding Vessel), UB 1 (Bright Eye)
•Comment: UB 1 (Bright Eye) is stimulated by staring with the eyes.

2.C. The Unicorn Turns Its Head to Look at the Moon:
• gathers *chi* in the upper warmer
• twists the body to compress the *chi* to the middle and lower warmer
• activate Governing *(Du)* channel by stretching and twisting the spine
• activate *Yang* Connecting *(Yang Qiao)* channel by stretching the ankles

•Extraordinary Channel: This movement stretches many channels but mainly the twisting of the spine stimulates *Yang* Connecting *(Yang Qiao)* at the back of the neck and Governing *(Du)*.
•Control Points: UB 62 (Expanding Vessel). UB 1 (Bright Eye) is stimulated by looking up.
•Comment: This is a good movement to do during a full moon because you connect with lunar energy.

2.D. Drawing the Precious Sword from Its Sheath:
• gathers *chi* in the trunk
• promotes *chi* flow in the Belt *(Dai Mai)* channel

> Advanced Students: Pull the energy up from all the main *yin* channels and *Yin* Connecting *(Yin Qiao)* and *Yin Regulating (Yin Wei)* extraordinary channels. Mainly this movement affects the Belt *(Dai Mai)*. This movement also promotes the flow of *chi* in the reproductive organs.

- Extraordinary Channels: Mainly Belt *(Dai Mai)*, also *Yin* Connecting *(Yin Qiao)* and *Yin* Regulating *(Yin Wei)*
- Control Points: GB 41 (Fallen Tear), K 6 (Illuminate the Sea), P 6 (Inner Gate)
- Comment: Good for blockages of the reproductive organs (*e.g.*, ovarian cysts). The Belt *(Dai Mai)* channel mainly engages in integration and smoother flow of energy in the waist area, affecting the liver/gall bladder and correspondingly the reproductive and gastrointestinal areas.

2.E. Moving the Mountain and Pouring Out the Sea:
- gathers *chi* from earth and trunk
- pushes *chi* up the spine and out of *Du* 20 (Hundred Meeting Point) at top of head
- stimulates SI 3 (Back Stream) on the hand (by turning out the palms and stretching the hands with the pinky fingers leading out) and activate Governing *(Du)* channel

> Advanced Students: This movement specifically stimulates the Yang Regulating *(Yang Wei)* channel which comes up the ear area, focusing on SJ 5 (External Gate).

- Extraordinary Channels: *Yang* Regulating *(Yang Wei)* and *Yang* Connecting *(Yang Qiao)*
- Control Point: SJ 5 (External Gate)
- Comment: This movement can improve strength and *chi*, and mainly activates defensive *chi* or the immune system.

Third Treasure:
Raising the Hands to Adjust the Stomach and Spleen

The Third Treasure uses the movement of raising your hands to pull the internal organs upward and support your interior. This Treasure contains only two important movements. Although they have the same purpose, they are different in order to help you make your internal organs strong, normal and function healthily. These movements specifically strengthen and balance your digestive and elimination systems.

Action: Stretch and massage the digestive organs
- enhances intestinal peristalsis
- benefits digestion
- strengthens the spleen's function in red and white cell production

3.A. The Jade Plate Receives the Morning Dew:
- gathers and focuses energy in the middle warmer
- promotes flow in the Belt (*Dai Mai*) channel
- cup formation of hand activates P 6 (Inner Gate) and *Yin* Regulating (*Yin Wei*) channel
- turn eyes downward to look at the hand as it sweeps down and across in front, to stimulate St 1 (Tears Receptacle) at the midpoint at the bottom of the eyes
- push *chi* out of *Du* 20 (Hundred Meeting Point) on top of head and activate the *Ren* 1 (*Yin* Meeting point) in the perineum by pushing down with the other palm

> Advanced Students: This movement works on the middle warmer, stomach and spleen. It also stretches the Governing (*Du*) channel. Raising the heels, in this case, stimulates GB 41 (Fallen Tear) and the Belt (*Dai Mai*) channel. Focus on P 6 (Inner Gate) during the stretch.

- Extraordinary Channels: *Yin* Regulating (*Yin Wei*), Belt (*Dai Mai*). Also stretches the Governing (*Du*).
- Control Points: P 6 (Inner Gate), GB 41 (Fallen Tear), SI 3 (Back Stream) (SI 3 is activated by turning out the palms and stretching the hands with the pinky fingers leading out)
- Comment: Good for people with digestive problems.

3.B. Looking at the Lotus Flower in the Clear Pond:

Keep the feet together. Feel the stretch and compression in the chest area and sides. The eyes contact the highest point of the heel and also GB 41 (Fallen Tear point). Looking down activates St 1 (Tears Receptacle).

Variation: Heel of one foot touches the high point of the arch of the other foot at Sp 4 (Heredity).

• stretches and massages the digestive organs in the trunk
• massage UB 10 (Jade Pillow) in the base of the neck by rubbing with wrist, stimulating P 6 (Inner Gate) and activating the *Yin Regulating (Yin Wei)* channel
• eyes focus on GB 41 (Fallen Tear)

Advanced Students: Connect the Vitality *(Chong Mai)* channel at Sp 4 (Heredity) with the Yin Regulating *(Yin Wei)* channel at P 6 (Inner Gate).

•Extraordinary Channels: Vitality *(Chong Mai)*, *Yin* Regulating *(Yin Wei,)* Belt *(Dai Mai)*
•Control Points: Sp 4 (Heredity) (foot arc), P 6 (Inner Gate), GB 41 (Fallen Tear)
•Comment: Good for digestive problems involving the stomach, spleen, liver and gall bladder.

Fourth Treasure:
Turning Your Head to Tonify the Nervous System

The Fourth Treasure works on the bridge between the head and the body, which is your neck. This section will help you accomplish the important transportation of *chi* from your head to your body and vice versa, so you will have smooth transportation between the two without a traffic jam!

Many people drive for a long time or work indoors all day doing office work. It is not muscular work at all, but their neck becomes very stiff. Having a stiff neck indicates that the transportation between the body and the head is not good, but you can easily correct this. Once it is corrected, you can avoid headaches (congestion in the head) because the transportation between the body and the head is easier. This Treasure helps you solve the partial congestion of energy in the head or neck area.

Action: Benefits the cerebral/spinal system, and the skeletal structural system.
- increases circulation to the brain
- strengthens cervical muscles and vertebra
- benefits the central nervous system
- removes fatigue from the brain
- improves the action of the nervous system on respiratory and circulatory systems
- strengthens ocular muscles
- increases the range of eyes

4.A. Turning the Head to Look at Your Star:
- gather energy
- one hand holds the other, with the middle or ring finger of the right hand pressing on SI 3 (Back Stream) on the left hand, activating the Governing (*Du*) channel while stretching and turning the neck

> Advanced Students: The hand position stimulates SI 3 (Back Stream). When you stretch the front of the neck, look up to stimulate UB 1 (Bright Eye point), which is the intersection point of the *Yin* Connecting (*Yin Qiao*) channel. K 6 is mildly stimulated through bending of the knees and ankles. Actively looking while twisting and bending will activate K 6 in the opposite direction than the direction you are facing.

- <u>Extraordinary Channels</u>: Activates the *Yin* Connecting (*Yin Qiao*: structural) and Governing (*Du*: cerebrospinal).
- <u>Control Points</u>: SI 3 (Back Stream), K 6 (Illuminate the Sea)
- <u>Comment</u>: This movement of turning the head across the front of the body and looking up stimulates both the spine (Governing, *Du*) and the *yin* aspect of the body (*Yin* Connecting, *Yin Qiao*).

4.B. Turning the Head to Contemplate Earth:
- circles gather energy in the kidneys
- middle or fourth finger stimulating SI 3 (Back Stream) of the other hand activates the Governing (*Du*) channel

• looking over shoulder at UB 62 (Expanding Vessel) activates the *Yang* Connecting (*Yang Qiao*) channel

> Advanced Students: The hand position stimulates SI 3 (Back Stream point). This exercise mainly activates *Yang* Connecting (*Yang Qiao*); the Governing (*Du*) Channel is also activated. Eyes look over the shoulder to UB 62 (Expanding Vessel); hands push down at the back opposite the lower *tan tien*.

•Extraordinary Channels: Mainly *Yang* Connecting (*Yang Qiao*) and Governing (*Du*)
•Control Point: UB 62 (Expanding Vessel)
Comment: This movement of turning the head across the back of the body stimulates the spine (Governing, *Du*) and *yang* aspect of the body *Yang* Connecting (*Yang Qiao*).

4.C. The Weeping Willow Shivers in the Early Morning Breeze:
This movement stimulates the major joints of the body.
• loosens all the joints
• relaxes the spinal column and soothes the nerves
• horizontal circles integrate all vertically flowing channels
• middle or ring finger stimulating SI 3 (Back Stream) of the other hand activates the Governing (*Du*) channel

> Advanced Students: Many channels pass through these major joints. Our joints, like bends in a river, are places where the flow can easily collect and stagnate. We need to exercise them regularly to keep them open and the channels free.

•Extraordinary Channel: Governing (*Du*)
•Control Point: SI 3 (Back Stream).
•Comment: This movement performed as part of the Eight Treasures gives a different benefit because the other movements have activated other channels. Although it is also done in the Warm-Up, it should not be skipped here.

Fifth Treasure:
Swaying the Spinal Column to Take Away Heart Fire

The Fifth Treasure helps strengthen your legs. The legs are like the main foundation of a house. Without a good foundation, the house will not be firmly supported. Similarly, it is necessary to strengthen the legs. Many people practice jogging or walking, which helps the body's circulation, but you need to do something for your legs. The two movements of the Fifth Treasure help you strengthen your legs and waist.

These movements also drain off excess "heart fire" or post-natal *chi* and store it in the kidneys. Facilitating this storage function is one reason why you must be sure to keep your lower back and rear tucked.

This Treasure exercises the *yang* aspect of the body. It is the tendency of *yang* energy to rise. The *yang* channels -- Governing *(Du)*, *Yang* Connecting *(Yang Qiao,)* *Yang* Regulating *(Yang Wei)* and Belt *(Dai Mai)* -- bring back excess *yang* for storage instead of wasting post-natal *chi* somewhere else. Having either too much heart fire (excessive *yang*) or *yin* depletion causes an imbalance in which the *chi* goes to and accumulates in the heart area, resulting in stress to the heart area. Too much heart fire disturbs the heart and manifests as derangement, mental disturbance, hysteria, restlessness, sleep disturbance and so forth. The squatting moves excessive fire from the heart to the Governing *(Du)*, *Yang* Connecting *(Yang Qiao)*, *Yang* Regulating *(Yang Wei)* and Belt *(Dai Mai)* channels.

Action: Enhances digestion and elimination.
• removes heart fire (mental distress)
• benefits all systems
• removes abnormal nervous tension
• benefits the smooth flow of energy through the spine and neck
• tightens the waist and the thigh

5.A. The Sleeping Lion Shifts Its Head and Awakens:

Gathers Heaven *chi* into the trunk. In the first part, squat and shift torso, look up and open eyes, resting side of head on back of the wrist at SJ 5 (External Gate).

First Part

> Advanced Students: The ear should touch SJ 5 (External Gate).
>
> For this movement it is ideal to do a perpendicular horse stance, which is very difficult. Riding horses will actually help develop this position. The ankle alignment is more important than aligning the knees and keeping the spine straight. Keeping the spine straight means twisting the trunk and not straining the back.

• Extraordinary Channels: *Yang* Connecting (*Yang Qiao*), *Yang* Regulating *(Yang Wei)*
• Control Points: UB 62 (Expanding Vessel), SJ 5 (External Gate)
• Comment: The combination of deep squatting and twisting stimulates UB 62 (Expanding Vessel) and the *Yang* Connecting *(Yang Qiao)*. You should feel a pulling sensation through the ankle area.
• connecting thumb and middle finger between movements connects *yin* and *yang* channels and activates P 6 (Inner Gate) and *Yin Regulating (Yin Wei)* channel to relieve anxiety and distress, storing excess energy in the kidneys.
• as an alternative, touch thumb to index finger (Large Intestine *yang* and Lung *yin*) to cause *yin* energy to pull the fire into storage.
• Gathers earth energy. In the second part, shift torso and place the elbow inside the knee. As you turn the torso, lean back against the knee with the arm between the head and knee.
• head rests on the hand, touching Back Stream (SI 3) point to GB 20 (Wind Pond Point) which activates Governing (*Du*) channel.

Second Part

> Advanced Students: GB 20 (Wind Point) on the back of the head touching SI 3 (Back Stream) connects the Governing *(Du)* with the *Yang* Connecting *(Yang Qiao)*. Looking up stimulates UB 1 (Bright Eye). Tailbone should be tucked in for maximum effect. This movement also works the stomach.

• Extraordinary Channels: *Yang* Connecting (*Yang Qiao*), Governing (*Du*)
• Control Points: UB 62 (Expanding Vessel), SI 3 (Back Stream)
• Comment: This movement drains the fire and stores the excess energy in the kidneys. Practicing this consistently will build stronger *chi*.

5.B. Lying Down to Watch the Constellations:
This movement opens the back, neck and head.
• grasping side of the chin with one hand over back of neck, and P 6 (Inner Gate) point touching UB 10 (Jade Pillow) on the base of the neck, activates the Urinary Bladder channel and *Yin* Regulating (*Yin Wei*) and Governing (*Du*) channels

> Advanced Students: The torso movement leads the head movement. This movement should be relaxing. It is easier to do if the feet are wider apart.

• Extraordinary Channels: *Yang* Connecting (*Yang Qiao*), *Yang* Regulating (*Yang Wei*), Governing (*Du*)
• Control Points: UB 62 (Expanding Vessel), SJ 5 (External Gate), SI 3 (Back Stream)
• Comment: There is a lot going on with this movement. There is activation of all the points around the ear. The Gall Bladder points in the neck, head and shoulders are stimulated with the twisting of the neck. The chest cavity is squeezed and twisted and H 1 (Highest Spring point, located at the center of the armpits) is activated to empty the heart fire and clear the chest, allowing the excess energy to be redistributed throughout the channel system.

Sixth Treasure:
Raising the Heels to Remove Physical and Mental Weakness
The Sixth Treasure helps awaken the brain, which in Traditional Chinese Medicine is called the "sea of marrow." Since the brain is protected by the skull, it is very hard to exercise. However, good breathing can bring it new oxygen, especially if you are well trained

or if you visit a spot like a mountain, ocean or waterfall. These places all have negative ions, which can immediately make you feel different.

The feeling of refreshment comes from breathing. The repetition of gently tapping the heels on the ground will stimulate your brain; when combined with breathing, this will help strengthen your brain energy. There is a limit to how many you should do of each of these two movements: no more than 7 to 9 times. There is no need to overdo them.

Action: Normalizes the central nervous system.
• vibrates all the organs
• increases brain's alertness
• removes fatigue
• refreshes the body

6.A. *Bringing the Stream Back to the Sea:*
Breathe through SI 3 (Back Stream point) into the lower *tan tien*; this means you are breathing through your hands. When you drop, hear the back of the teeth chatter.
• raises the water energy (Kidney channel) by raising the heel and stimulating K 1 (Rushing Spring) point in the bottom of the feet
• encourages energy into lower *tan tien*
• stimulates the vital force
• rocking the spine activates the Governing (*Du*) channel

> Advanced Students: As you come down, you should feel the spinal vibration up to the top of the head to *Du* 20 (Hundred Meeting Point) Take your time; this is a meditative movement.

• Extraordinary Channels: Governing (*Du*), *Yang* Connecting *(Yang Qiao)*
• Control Points: SI 3 (Back Stream), UB 62 (Expanding Vessel), K 6 (Illuminate the Sea)
• Comment: This movement stimulates a process of awakening; it is very important. It stimulates and awakens the body.

6.B. Pumping the Water from the Origin of the Fountain:

Use the middle or fourth finger to hold onto K 6 (Illuminate the Sea) on the inside ankle, and the thumb to hold UB 62 (Expanding Vessel) below the outer ankle; breathe while focusing on these two points. Use a pulling upward motion to lift with the inhale.

• stimulates the *Yang* Connecting (*Yang Qiao*) channel by grabbing the heel with the thumb pressing on UB 62 (Expanding Vessel)

• vibrates all organs and rocks the Governing (*Du*) channel

> Advanced Students: This is a very good visualization: as you go up and down, and every time you come down, you are stimulating K 1 (Rushing Spring point) like water coming out of "The Bubbling Spring," which is another translation of the name of this point. You can consider this bubbling spring to be the "origin of the fountain." The force mostly comes from the upward pulling or lifting, and you are helping enhance it when you grab the ankles. This movement gives your heels a very good workout and activates UB 62 (Expanding Vessel) and K 6 (Illuminate the Sea).

• Extraordinary Channels: Mainly Governing (*Du*) and *Yang* Connecting (*Yang Qiao*)

• Control Points: UB 62 (Expanding Vessel), K 6 (Illuminate the Sea)

• Comment: After you have practiced this movement long enough, there is a phenomenon of *chi* like a hover craft. There actually is *chi* ejecting out of the K 1 (Rushing Spring) point, and you really can have fun with it like a leap frog. (Yes, I do the movement a little different from the way my father does it!) But remember, just do 7 or 9 repetitions each time.

Seventh Treasure:
Tightening the Tendons to Reinforce Yourself

The Seventh Treasure will help you gain strength. In general, modern people who are office workers or indoor workers do not use force any more. It is okay not to use force, but we should not let our muscles atrophy or become dormant. Our systems are weakened by not having enough exercise, physical movement or physical work. Thus this Treasure is very useful.

The purpose of being strong, however, is not so you can fight with people. In this Treasure, you fight with the air. You create internal pressure, and you allow the pressure to awaken your internal strength. You exercise the potential of the force to support your health and self-discipline.

Action: Strengthens and balances the tendomuscular, cardiovascular, and the liver and gall bladder systems.

- strengthens bones and tendons
- enhances circulation of oxygen and blood
- prevents joint degeneration
- excites the cerebral cortex
- benefits the liver

7.A. Pushing Down the Fierce Tiger:

Pull up the energy from the *Yin* Regulating *(Yin Wei)*. Push down into the lower *tan tien*, gathering the energy into the *tan tien* instead of scattering it through your arms. Slightly raise the heels when you drop and "push down the tiger."
- brings *yin chi* up the inside of the legs
- compresses *chi* into the *tan tien* and to the perineum by bending the wrist to push down, activating P 6 (Inner Gate) point and *Yin* Regulating *(Yin Wei)* channel

> Advanced Students: The tiger sequence works with the more active *yang* energies simply by having quick, active movements. Make yourself large and expansive during this sequence.

- Extraordinary Channel: *Yin* Regulating *(Yin Wei)*
- Control Point: P 6 (Inner Gate)
- Comment: This movement is also good for the kidneys.

7.B. The Tiger Grabs Its Prey:

- gathers *chi* from the Conception *(Ren)* channel and brings it to the arms, bending at the wrists and activating Lu 7 (Branching Crevice)

> Advanced Students: This is a grabbing movement. There is a definite tightening in the fingers, elbows, wrists and hands, but the *chi* manifests in the fingers or "claws." P 6 (Inner Gate) is activated by hands and inner forearms.

• Extraordinary Channel: *Yin* Regulating *(Yin Wei)* and Conception *(Ren)*
• Control Points: P 6 (Inner Gate), Lu 7 (Branching Crevice)
• Comment: You can do this movement in either a gentle or coarse projection of *chi* from the *tan tien*. Continuous practice should evolve into a gentle type of movement instead of a rough expression of *chi*. Since we are earthbound creatures, the connection of the *chi* really comes up from the ground, rising into the *tan tien* and to the fingers.

7.C. Clench the Teeth, Widen the Eyes and Strike in the Four Directions:
• gathers energy in the trunk into the Belt *(Dai Mai)* channel
• widening the eyes excites the cerebral cortex and stimulates the liver
• clenching the teeth stimulates the kidneys
• grabbing the ground underneath by flexing the big toes stimulates the Liver channel

> Advanced Students: Good for draining off excess liver *chi* or negative *chi*. If you are feeling angry, you can work off your excess liver *chi* in a very constructive way by punching toward a tree (wood element) which is the receptor. Do not actually punch the tree!

• Extraordinary Channel: Belt *(Dai Mai)*
• Control Point: GB 41 (Fallen Tear)

•Comment: My brother and I used to practice punching toward a pail of water without touching it. After six months of persistent practice we could see the water move, so we knew that there was *chi* coming out of the hands. That is a martial art, which is not what we teach, but there definitely is a circulation of energy into the hands which can be gathered and redirected. What we teach is how this energy can be used constructively through the internal arts for beneficial health therapy.

7.D. The Tiger Gathers its Energy and Crouches:
The previous movements have been expansive. Now you move to gather and accumulate the *chi*.
• packs *chi* into the lower *tan tien*

•Extraordinary Channel: Vitality *(Chong Mai)*
•Control Point: Sp 4 (Heredity)
•Comment: Feel the movement. Guide the *chi* with your mind, but do not intellectualize it.

Eighth Treasure:
Grabbing the Ankles to Strengthen Your Vital Force
The Eighth Treasure has the largest number of movements. This group of movements basically works on the lower part of the body. The *Tao Teh Ching* says, "The lower part of the body is the foundation of the upper body." The lower part of the body starts with the kidneys and reproductive organs. You do not need to be admired as a rooster or a queen bee! However, you still need to have that strength for your good health. The Eighth Treasure not only helps you generate reproductive energy, but it also helps you attain a higher level and transform the reproductive energy through sublimation.

Action: The Crane movements in this Treasure primarily develop the endocrine glands, cerebral-spinal system, bones and tendons, and also aid digestion and elimination.

• strengthens the lumbar muscles and the leg muscles
• benefits the lower organs, especially the kidneys and bladder
• rejuvenates the reproductive systems

- improves adrenal functions
- increases flexibility
- strengthens vitality

8.A. The White Crane Washes Its Wing Feathers:

Before the twists to each side, you can bend the back up and down while pumping the arms which stimulates the energy of the Belt (*Dai Mai*) and the Governing (*Du*) channels.
- twisting up and pulling up on kidneys stimulates and increases kidney energy (*yang* aspect)
- twisting down and pulling helps the kidneys and lower organs (*yin* aspect)
- thumbs on UB 10 (Jade Pillow); fingers interlaced with little finger of each hand touching SI 3 (Back Stream) of the other hand

- Extraordinary Channels: Belt (*Dai Mai*), Governing (*Du*), Yang Connecting (*Yang Qiao*)
- Control Points: GB 41 (Fallen Tear), SI 3 (Back Stream), UB 62 (Expanding Vessel)
- Comment: This movement provides good stimulation to the kidneys.

8. B. The White Crane Turns its Head to Look Up:

Grasp the knees with the hands to stimulate the points around the knees. Keep the spine and neck straight as you turn the head; to do this, it helps to keep the chin slightly tucked.
- turning the neck stimulates the Governing (*Du*) channel
- looking up stimulates UB 1 (Bright Eye)

> Advanced Students: This stretch engages a different set of muscles and channels than other neck stretches.

- Extraordinary Channels: Yang Connecting (*Yang Qiao*), Governing (*Du*), Belt (*Dai Mai*)
- Control Points: UB 62 (Expanding Vessel), SI 3 (Back Stream), GB 41 (Fallen Tear)
- Comment: Feel the *chi* in the spine moving freely through the neck and out of *Du* 20 Hundred Meeting Point).

8.C. The White Crane Twists Its Body to Look Up:

One hand grabs the opposite ankle, around the K 6 (Illuminate the Sea) and UB 62 (Expanding Vessel) points.
• thumb pressing on K 6 (Illuminate the Sea), activating the *Yin* Connecting (*Yin Qiao*) channel

---

Advanced Students: Develop a full body twist so that your upper shoulder is turned back, giving you an unobstructed view looking straight up. You can slightly pull with the hand holding the ankle, and push with the hand holding the knee. With practice this movement allows the whole spine to open up.

•Extraordinary Channels: Belt *(Dai Mai)*, Governing *(Du)*, *Yin* Connecting *(Yin Qiao)*
•Control Points: GB 41 (Fallen Tear), SI 3 (Back Stream), K 6 (Illuminate the Sea)
•Comment: Feel the *chi* at the kidneys as you twist.

8.D. The White Crane Sharpens Its Beak:

The chin touching the knee, compressing the trunk massages the abdominal viscera.
• thumbs on UB 10 (Jade Pillow) point while hands are behind head; fingers interlaced with little finger of each hand touching SI 3 (Back Stream) of the other hand
• hands touching GB 41 (Fallen Tear) activates Belt *(Dai Mai)* channel

---

Advanced Students: Put your hands on your feet or next to the *Yang* Connecting *(Yang Qiao)* channel.

•Extraordinary Channels: Governing *(Du)*, Belt *(Dai Mai)*, *Yang* Connecting *(Yang Qiao)*
•Control Points: SI 3 (Back Stream), GB 41 (Fallen Tear), UB 62 (Expanding Vessel)
•Comment: Feel the *chi* in the waist at *Belt (Dai Mai)* and down the leg to GB 41 (Fallen Tear).

8.E. The White Crane Strengthens Its Vital Force:
Compressing the trunk massages the abdominal viscera.
- thumbs touch UB 10 (Jade Pillow) while hands are behind head
- hands touching GB 41 (Fallen Tear) activates Belt (*Dai Mai*) channel
- then hands should be on the feet or touching ankles at K 6 (Illuminate the Sea) and UB 62 (Expanding Vessel)

> Advanced Students: Note the continued progression of the movements in working with the organ systems and channels. In the previous movement, the stretch related to the *Yang* Connecting (*Yang Qiao*) channel (among others). In this movement the stretch relates (among others) to the *Yin* Connecting (*Yin Qiao*) channel. While the hands touch at both K 6 (Illuminate the Sea) and UB 62 (Expanding Vessel point), it is K 6 (Illuminate the Sea) that is among the control points in this movement.

- Extraordinary Channels: Conception (*Ren*), Belt (*Dai Mai*), Yin Connecting (*Yin Qiao*)
- Control Points: Lu 7 (Branching Crevice Point), GB 41 (Fallen Tear point), K 6 (Illuminate the Sea)
- Comment: Be cautious in stretching the lumbar if you have low back problems; perform the bending in graduated fashion. Over time you should be able to touch the nose to the knees.

8.F. The White Crane Stretches Its Legs Behind and Forward:
- roots the energy solidly on standing leg
- gathers *chi* into K 1 (Rushing Spring) point

> Advanced Students: This is the only movement in the entire Eight Treasures in which you hold your breath. You do it when your leg is stretched straight out behind.
>
> When the leg is stretched out forward, exhale when descending and inhale when ascending.

• Extraordinary Channels: Conception *(Ren)*, Belt *(Dai Mai)*, *Yin* Connecting *(Yin Qiao)*
• Control Points: Lu 7 (Branching Crevice), GB 41 (Fallen Tear), K 6 (Illuminate the Sea)
• Comment: You will want to practice this movement regularly for strengthening the legs. Also, if you will be teaching and demonstrating this movement (for example, as a teacher or assistant teacher), you must work on this movement to demonstrate it well.

8.G. The White Crane Guards the Plum Flower Proudly Standing Alone on the Cold Mountain:

This movement unites water and fire energy because the knee is part of the Kidney/water system, and the chest is part of the Heart/fire system.
• *chi* in K 1 (Rushing Spring)
• knee touches heart area, connecting fire and water
• hands touch UB 62 (Expanding Vessel) and K 6 (Illuminate the Sea) by grabbing the ankles
• tighten sphincter muscle during inhale

> Advanced Students: Raise your heels to further stimulate the K 1 (Rushing Spring) point. This is also good for developing balance.

• Extraordinary Channels: *Yin* Connecting *(Yin Qiao)*, *Yang* Connecting *(Yang Qiao)*, *Yin* Regulating *(Yin Wei)*, *Yang* Regulating *(Yang Wei)*
• Control Points: K 6 (Illuminate the Sea), UB 62 (Expanding Vessel point), P 6 (Inner Gate point), SJ 5 (External Gate point)
• Comment: This movement helps to activate energy from the perineum.

8.H. The White Crane Limbers Its Wings:

• twisting at the waist stimulates abdominal viscera and activates the Belt *(Dai Mai)* channel

> Advanced Students: The hands locking together in back over the shoulder blades massages UB 43 (Deep Interior) between the shoulder blades.

•Extraordinary Channels: Belt *(Dai Mai)*, *Yang* Connecting *(Yang Qiao)*
•Control Points: GB 41 (Fallen Tear), UB 62 (Expanding Vessel)
•Comment: The objective of this movement is to open and stretch the arms, shoulders, shoulder blades, which all together would be our wings if we were white cranes.

8.I. The Dragon Flies Throughout the Heavens:
Be sure that as you do the circles, you do them with the waist rather than the arms. Don't let the *chi* scatter away from you through empty movement of the arms. Instead, use your waist turns, inhales and focus to gather your *chi*.
• circulates *chi* throughout the body and the extremities
• brings *chi* back to the lower *tan tien*

> Advanced Students: Consciously pull the gathered *chi* into your *tan tien*.

•Extraordinary Channels: All eight channels
•Control Points: All eight Master (Control) Points
•Comment: This movement integrates all the *chi* throughout the body. We take the *chi* we gather from the environment and Heaven and pull it into the *tan tien*.

Gathering the *Chi* (Standing Meditation)
The standing meditation at the conclusion of the Eight Treasures is very important. If you do it longer than 2 minutes, it brings all the gathered *chi* back to the lower *tan tien*.

7
Questions and Answers
Q: After concluding my practice, is it all right for me to do sitting meditation instead of standing meditation?

A: Yes, assuming you have returned the *chi* to the lower *tan tien*. You must do this return of *chi* first.

Q: After I finish doing the Eight Treasures, I cannot concentrate well when I go back to the office and start to work. Am I doing it right?

A: It means you neglected to gather your *chi* back to the *tan tien*, the storage center. Quietly bring your focus and *chi* back to the *tan tien* with a standing meditation. Part of the practice is to collect the moved energy back into storage.

Also, are you practicing during your lunch hour? Remember that noon is the one time you should not do it, because *yang* energy is at its fullest. At noon you can just take a break from work and perhaps walk a little to help prevent congesting *chi* in your head at that time.

Q: You have mentioned that chi *or energy is circulated within and outside of the body when doing the Eight Treasures. What type of energy is circulated? Nutritive energy? Post-natal energy? Pre-natal energy? Universal energy? Physical energy?*

A: All energy is collectively circulated.

Q: What does it mean exactly to refine chi *by doing the Eight Treasures? When I was young, I worked in a sugar-refining factory. I know what refining sugar is about: taking out impurities and making the sugar very pure. But what exactly are we talking about when we talk about refining* chi?

A: Thank you for your analogy. The process of refinement is the same no matter what is being refined. You take out the negative aspect, which is whatever you don't want, and you concentrate the positive aspect. That is refinement.

In energy cultivation and refinement, achieved ones speak of pure *yang*. The ultimate goal of a cultivator is to have pure *yang* in his or her body. Pure *yang*, in the context of human energy, means the pure, good, positive *chi*. If we look at *chi* as having both an informational-message aspect and a carrier-substance aspect, we understand that we can make changes in the substantial aspect of the *chi* by directing the informational aspect of the *chi*.

You refine your thoughts, behavior and actions. This type of self-refinement is taking away undesirable destructive *chi* from your body and adding constructive/positive influences so that you can be a totally positive being of pure *yang* energy.

When you cultivate *chi*, it is important to live a virtuous life on a daily basis. Virtue is positive function or maximum fulfillment in your life so that every thought and action that is projected in the form of *chi* or received in the form of *chi* is positive. If you continue to contaminate yourself, in your thoughts for example, your *chi* would contain that.

As you purify and concentrate your *chi* as positive *yang* energy, it becomes imperative to guard against negative contamination of any sort. An analogy of the need to protect your effort can be demonstrated by aquifers in nature. How do you think nature produces pure water for your consumption? After rain falls to the earth, it becomes muddy or subject to contamination from many factors. It takes various processes and many steps of filtration through mother earth to become a pure collection of water suitable for good use. It takes thousands of years to gather the purest water in a natural underground aquifer, but that purity can be destroyed by leakage of various fertilizers or pesticides and toxic chemicals into the soil. Similarly in spiritual development, what took so long to build can be ruined in one day of misconduct. You need to purify your personal energy as water is purified for drinking.

Q: Is the mind really a source of power?

A: Through physics and parapsychology, scientists have just begun to realize that the mind can indeed alter functions of the body through concentration and programming. I repeat, "Thoughts are louder than thunder." Wherever you send your thoughts, you send your energy. So you need to be careful to make your thoughts serve you well.

Your mind can be a good servant, but not a good master. You have learned that the mind can properly guide the body, so you might think that the mind should be the master. However, there is something more subtle which has more wisdom and more power. It is your spirit.

The Eight Treasures not only harmonize your *yin* and *yang* energies, they also integrate your body, mind and spirit. Just as you nourish and strengthen your body, and your mind, you can also nourish and strengthen your spirit. You can use the Eight Treasures for this purpose, and you can learn a lot more in the process of doing it.

The Sleeping Lion Shifts Its Head and Awakens
(Figure 73)

Chapter 8

Learning Through Teaching the Eight Treasures

Doing the Eight Treasures is an excellent way to further your spiritual growth. You may also be interested in additional avenues for growth, or in rendering spiritual service to others by promoting the healthy lifestyle of the Integral Way. In doing so, not only will you enhance your own self-development with the Eight Treasures, you will also learn about deep spiritual leadership, management of your life being and guiding the spiritual dynamics of groups of healthy individuals.

The Universal Society of the Integral Way (USIW) offers membership to anyone who is interested in the Integral Way. All people including students or those who are in study groups are welcome to participate as members. This provides opportunities for continued learning about complete physical, mental and spiritual health, and the healthy expression of a natural integral life. It also provides a network to share with others in learning, growing and volunteering service.

The USIW also certifies mentors as teachers to assist students and to teach future mentors. Through the USIW mentorship program, individuals who live with the model of the Integral Way of life may become recognized as mentors to teach or provide other service at a higher level of commitment. Members who have studied the Integral Way may become mentors, and if they are proficient at practicing the Eight Treasures they may be certified to teach the Eight Treasures.

The programs for members and mentors are coordinated and administered by mentors who teach through the USIW. Members and mentors learn the Integral Way of life through such avenues as the self-study program and the Correspondence Course offered by the College of Tao and the Integral Way; classes, seminars and study groups (coordinated through the USIW); and their own spiritual self-cultivation.

Other mentors do not teach directly, yet provide service in other ways. Some examples of their activities are assisting with book promotions and publications, producing teaching material, volunteering their other talents and skills, and creating and supporting study groups.

The USIW publishes a quarterly newsletter with news of member and mentor activities, teachings by Hua-Ching Ni, Daoshing Ni, and Maoshing Ni, new publications and videos, cultural and social events, and other items of interest. It is available by subscription, and is also provided to all members and mentors.

If you would like information about these activities or becoming a member, please write to the Universal Society of the Integral Way, P.O. Box 28993, Atlanta, GA 30358-0993 (USA) or call 770-392-9605. You may also use the form at the back of this book to request information.

(Information on publications is available from SevenStar Communications, 1314 Second Street, Santa Monica, CA 90401 USA, telephone number (310) 576-1901, fax number (310) 917-2267, or use the order form at the back of this book.)

About the Author, Maoshing Ni

Maoshing Ni, L.A.C., Dipl.C.H., D.O.M., Ph.D. is the author of *The Tao of Nutrition* (now in its second edition), *Chinese Herbology Made Easy*, and *The Yellow Emperor's Classic of Medicine - a New Translation of the Neijing Su Wen with Commentary*. These are also used as textbooks at Yo San University of Traditional Chinese Medicine. He is featured in the Eight Treasures™ videotape, Self-Healing *Chi Gong* videotape, has authored several audio and video programs on *Chi Gong, T'ai Chi Ch'uan* and Eight Treasures, and co-authored *The Golden Message* with Dr. Daoshing Ni.

As a 38th-generation medical practitioner in his family, Dr. Maoshing Ni has received extensive training in traditional healing arts and medicine from his father, Hua-Ching Ni, and many other achieved teachers. Dr. Ni maintains a busy private practice in Santa Monica, California, where he also instructs at Yo San University of Traditional Chinese Medicine, which he co-founded with his family.

About Hua-Ching Ni

Hua-Ching Ni is the author of over forty books in English on philosophy, Chinese medicine, *T'ai Chi* Movement, Taoist meditation and related subjects. His practice of Chinese medicine and herbology spanned over five decades in China, Taiwan and the U.S. He was chosen as a youth to spend years living with and learning from Taoist Masters in the high mountains of mainland China. He was raised in a long family tradition of healing and spirituality that is carried on today in Santa Monica by his two sons, Drs. Daoshing and Maoshing Ni.

The Dragon Flies Throughout the Heavens
(Figure 74)

For Further Information

It is said that the highest essence of truth is used for examining one's own mind and body. - Chuang Tzu

Related materials of interest to practitioners of the Eight Treasures, listed by topic. These materials are available through your local bookstore or SevenStar Communications.

Breathing
Crane Style Chi Gong, By Daoshing Ni, Chapter III, Part 3: "Breathing Regulation"

Power of Natural Healing by Hua-Ching Ni, Chapter 10: "Breathing Reaches Soul"

Strength From Movement: Mastering Chi by Hua-Ching Ni, with Daoshing Ni and Maoshing Ni, Chapter 7, "The Breath of Life"

Chi
Book of Changes and the Unchanging Truth (I Ching) by Hua-Ching Ni, Chapter 8: "Natural Energy in Human Life"

Guide to Inner Light by Hua-Ching Ni, Chapter 2, pp. 36-50 and 98-102 for discussion on cultivating *chi*

Internal Alchemy: The Natural Way to Immortality by Hua-Ching Ni, "Concluding Instruction," for description of the movement of *chi*

Life and Teachings of Two Immortals, Volume II: Chen Tuan by Hua-Ching Ni, Chapter 4: "Internal Energy Conducting and Orbit Circulation"

8,000 Years of Wisdom, Book II by Hua-Ching Ni, Chapter 60: "The Main Principles of Cultivating *Chi*"

Strength From Movement: Mastering Chi by Hua-Ching Ni, with Daoshing Ni and Maoshing Ni, especially Chapter 6, "The Basis of Physical Art: *Chi*"

Tao, The Subtle Universal Law and the Integral Way of Life by Hua-Ching Ni

Chi Gong (Chi Kung)
Crane Style Chi Gong Videotape (VHS) by Dr. Daoshing Ni (and accompanying book)

Life and Teachings of Two Immortals, Volume I: Kou Hong by Hua-Ching Ni, Chapter 4, pp. 69-74 for discussion of *chi gong* and *t'ai chi*

Self-Healing Chi Gong Videotape (VHS) by Dr. Maoshing Ni

Strength From Movement: Mastering Chi by Hua-Ching Ni, with Daoshing Ni and Maoshing Ni, especially Chapter 2, "Choosing the Exercise that is Right for You," Section 1: "Comparing the Different Types"

Diet
8,000 Years of Wisdom, Book I by Hua-Ching Ni, Chapter 35: "Introduction to Diet," Chapter 36: "Foods in General" and Chapter 37: "The Healing Properties of Food"

Integral Nutrition: Nourishing Your Healthy Life (booklet)

Tao of Nutrition by Dr. Maoshing Ni and Cathy McNease

Chinese Vegetarian Delights by Lily Chuang and Cathy McNease

101 Vegetarian Delights by Lily Chuang and Cathy McNease

Eight Treasures
Eight Treasures Videotape (VHS) by Maoshing Ni, Ph.D.

Strength From Movement: Mastering Chi by Hua-Ching Ni, with Daoshing Ni and Maoshing Ni, Chapter 3: "Description of Each Type of Exercise" for a brief description of the Eight Treasures and comparison with other types of *chi* exercises

Exercise (Other *Chi* Exercises):
Attune Your Body with Dao-In Videotape (VHS) and book by Hua-Ching Ni

Strength From Movement: Mastering Chi by Hua-Ching Ni, with Daoshing Ni and Maoshing Ni for information on many different types of gentle physical arts.

Health and Healing:
Chinese Herbology Made Easy by Dr. Maoshing Ni

Crane Style Chi Gong, Chapter 1: *"Chi Gong* as a Medical Therapy"

Tao, the Subtle Universal Law by Hua-Ching Ni, Chapter 3: "The Human Body and Universal Law" and Chapter 4: "The Art of Preserving Health"

The Power of Natural Healing by Hua-Ching Ni

The Yellow Emperor's Classic of Medicine - A New Translation of the Neijing Su Wen with Commentary, by Maoshing Ni

Meditation
Attune Your Body with Dao-In (book) by Hua-Ching Ni, Chapter 8, pp. 94-106.

Enlightenment: Mother of Spiritual Independence by Hua-Ching Ni, Chapter 5: "How to Use Meditation to Attain Your Enlightenment"

Eternal Light by Hua-Ching Ni, Chapter 10: "Guidance for Deep Meditation"

Life and Teachings of Two Immortals, Volume I: Kou Hong by Hua-Ching Ni, Chapter 3: "Instruction for Good Meditation"

Life and Teachings of Two Immortals, Volume II: Chen Tuan by Hua-Ching Ni, Chapter 3: "Essential Guidelines for Meditation and Sleeping Meditation"

Spring Thunder: Awaken the Hibernating Power of Life by Hua-Ching Ni

Story of Two Kingdoms by Hua-Ching Ni, "Taoist Indoor Meditation," pp. 106-111.

Mind
Key to Good Fortune by Hua-Ching Ni

Mysticism: Empowering the Spirit Within by Hua-Ching Ni

Workbook for Spiritual Development of All People by Hua-Ching Ni, Chapter 3: "Work to Improve the Quality of Your Mind"

Strength From Movement: Mastering Chi by Hua-Ching Ni, with Daoshing Ni and Maoshing Ni, Chapter 8, "Mind: The Sensitive Partner"

Spiritual Classics
Attaining Unlimited Life (The Book of Chuang Tzu) by Hua-Ching Ni

The Book of Changes and the Unchanging Truth (I Ching) by Hua-Ching Ni

Complete Works of Lao Tzu by Hua-Ching Ni, containing the *Tao Teh Ching* and the *Hua Hu Ching*

Esoteric Tao Teh Ching by Hua-Ching Ni

Yin and Yang
Tao, the Subtle Universal Law by Hua-Ching Ni, Chapter 1

All books, booklets and videotapes are available from SevenStar Communications. Complete descriptions and order form may be found on the following pages.

Drawing the Precious Sword From Its Sheath
(Figure 75)

Teachings of the Universal Way by Hua-Ching Ni

NEW RELEASES

From Diversity to Unity: Return to the One Spiritual Source - This book encourages individuals to go beyond the theological boundary to rediscover their own spiritual nature with guidance offered by Hua-Ching Ni from his personal achievement, exploration, and self-cultivation. This work can help people unlock the spiritual treasures of the universe and light the way to a life of internal and external harmony and fulfillment. ISBN 0-937064-87-4 PAPERBACK, 200 P $15.95

Spring Thunder: Awaken the Hibernating Power of Life - Humans need to be periodically awakened from a spiritual hibernation in which the awareness of life's reality is deeply forgotten. To awaken your deep inner life, this book offers the practice of Natural Meditation, the enlightening teachings of Yen Shi, and Master Ni's New Year Message. BSPRI 0-937064-77-7 PAPERBACK, 168 P $12.95

The Eight Treasures: Energy Enhancement Exercise - by Maoshing Ni, Ph. D. The Eight Treasures is an ancient system of energy enhancing movements based on the natural motion of the universe. It can be practiced by anyone at any fitness level, is non-impact, simple to do, and appropriate for all ages. It is recommended that this book be used with its companion videotape. BEIGH 0-937064-55-6 Paperback 208p $17.95

The Universal Path of Natural Life - The way to make your life enduring is to harmonize with the nature of the universe. By doing so, you expand beyond your limits to reach universal life. This book is the third in the series called *The Course for Total Health*. BUNIV 0-937064-76-9 PAPERBACK, 104P $9.50

Power of Positive Living How do you know if your spirit is healthy? You do not need to be around sickness to learn what health is. When you put aside the cultural and social confusion around you, you can rediscover your true self and restore your natural health. This is the second book of *The Course for Total Health*. BPOWE 0-937064-90-4 PAPERBACK 80P $8.50

The Gate to Infinity - People who have learned spiritually through years without real progress will be thoroughly guided by the important discourse in this book. Master Ni also explains Natural Meditation. Editors recommend that all serious spiritual students who wish to increase their spiritual potency read this one. BGATE 0-937064-68-8 PAPERBACK 208P $13.95

The Yellow Emperor's Classic of Medicine - by Maoshing Ni, Ph.D. The *Neijing* is one of the most important classics of Taoism, as well as the highest authority on traditional Chinese medicine. Written in the form of a discourse between Yellow Emperor and his ministers, this book contains a wealth of knowledge on holistic medicine and how human life can attune itself to receive natural support. BYELLO 1-57062-080-6 PAPERBACK 316P $16.00

Self-Reliance and Constructive Change - Natural spiritual reality is independent of concept. Thus dependence upon religious convention, cultural notions and political ideals must be given up to reach full spiritual potential. The Declaration of Spiritual Independence affirms spiritual self-authority and true wisdom as the highest attainments of life. This is the first book in *The Course for Total Health*. BSELF 0-937064-85-8 PAPERBACK 64P $7.00

Concourse of All Spiritual Paths - All religions, in spite of their surface difference, in their essence return to the great oneness. Hua-Ching Ni looks at what traditional religions offer us today and suggests how to go beyond differences to discover the depth of universal truth. BCONC 0-937064-61-0 PAPERBACK 184P $15.95.

PRACTICAL LIVING

The Key to Good Fortune: Refining Your Spirit - Straighten Your Way *(Tai Shan Kan Yin Pien)* and The Silent Way of Blessing *(Yin Chia Wen)* are the main guidance for a mature, healthy life. Spiritual improvement can be an integral part of realizing a Heavenly life on Earth. BKEYT 0-937064-39-4 PAPERBACK 144P $12.95

Harmony - The Art of Life - The emphasis in this book is on creating harmony within ourselves so that we can find it in relationships with other people and with our environment. BHARM 0-937064-37-8 PAPERBACK 208P $14.95

Ageless Counsel for Modern Life - Following the natural organization of the *I Ching*, Hua-Ching Ni has woven inspired commentaries to each of the 64 hexagrams. Taken alone, they display an inherent wisdom which is both personal and profound. BAGEL 0-937064-50-5 PAPERBACK 256P $15.95.

Strength From Movement: Mastering Chi - by Hua-Ching Ni, Daoshing Ni and Maoshing Ni. - *Chi*, the vital power of life, can be developed and cultivated within yourself to help support your healthy, happy life. This book gives the deep reality of different useful forms of *chi* exercise and which types are best for certain types of people. Includes samples of several popular exercises. BSTRE 0-937064-73-4 PAPERBACK WITH 42 PHOTOGRAPHS 256P $16.95.

8,000 Years of Wisdom, Volume I and II - This two-volume set contains a wealth of practical, down-to-earth advice given to students over a five-year period. Volume I includes 3 chapters on dietary guidance. Volume II devotes 7 chapters to sex and pregnancy topics. VOLUME I: BWIS1 0-937064-07-6 PAPERBACK 236P $12.50 • VOLUME II: BWIS2 0-937064-08-4 PAPERBACK 241P $12.50

The Time is Now for a Better Life and a Better World - What is the purpose of personal spiritual achievement if not to serve humanity by improving the quality of life for everyone? Hua-Ching Ni offers his vision of humanity's dilemma and what can be done about it. BTIME 0-937064-63-7 PAPERBACK 136P $10.95

Spiritual Messages from a Buffalo Rider, A Man of Tao - This book is a collection of talks from Hua-Ching Ni's world tour and offers valuable insights into the interaction between a compassionate spiritual teacher and his students from many countries around the world. BSPIR 0-937064-34-3 PAPERBACK 242P $12.95

Golden Message - by Daoshing and Maoshing Ni - This book is a distillation of the teachings of the Universal Way of Life as taught by the authors' father, Hua-Ching Ni. Included is a complete program of study for students and teachers of the Way. BGOLD 0-937064-36-x PAPERBACK 160P $11.95

Moonlight in the Dark Night - This book contains wisdom on how to control emotions, including how to manage love relationships so that they do not impede one's spiritual achievement. BMOON 0-937064-44-0 PAPERBACK 168P $12.95

SPIRITUAL DEVELOPMENT

Life and Teaching of Two Immortals, Volume 1: Kou Hong - A master who achieved spiritual ascendancy in 363 A.D., Kou Hong was an achieved master in the art of alchemy. His teachings apply the Universal Way to business, politics, emotions, human relationships, health and destiny. BLIF1 0-937064-47-5 PAPERBACK 176P $12.95.

Life and Teaching of Two Immortals, Volume 2: Chen Tuan - Chen Tuan was an achieved master who was famous for the foreknowledge he attained through deep study of the *I Ching* and for his unique method of "sleeping cultivation." This book also includes important details about the microcosmic meditation and mystical instructions from the "Mother of Li Mountain." BLIF2 0-937064-48-3 PAPERBACK 192P $12.95

The Way, the Truth and the Light - *now available in paperback!* - Presented in light, narrative form, this inspiring story unites Eastern and Western beliefs as it chronicles a Western prophet who journeys to the East in pursuit of further spiritual guidance. BLIGH1 0-937064-56-4 PAPERBACK 232P $14.95 • BLIGH2 0-937064-67-X HARDCOVER 232P $22.95

The Mystical Universal Mother - Hua-Ching Ni responds to the questions of his female students through the example of his mother and other historical and mythical women. He focuses on the feminine aspect of both sexes and on the natural relationship between men and women. BMYST 0-937064-45-9 PAPERBACK 240P $14.95

Eternal Light - Dedicated to Yo San Ni, a renowned healer and teacher, and father of Hua-Ching Ni. An intimate look at the lifestyle of a spiritually centered family. BETER 0-937064-38-6 PAPERBACK 208P $14.95

Quest of Soul - How to strengthen your soul, achieve spiritual liberation, and unite with the universal soul. A detailed discussion of the process of death is also included. BQUES 0-937064-26-2 PAPERBACK 152P $11.95

Nurture Your Spirits - Spirits are the foundation of our being. Hua-Ching Ni reveals the truth about "spirits" based on his personal cultivation and experience, so that you can nurture your own spirits. BNURT 0-937064-32-7 PAPERBACK 176P $12.95

Internal Alchemy: The Natural Way to Immortality - Ancient spiritually achieved ones used alchemical terminology metaphorically to disguise personal internal energy transformation. This book offers the prescriptions that help sublimate your energy. BALCH 0-937064-51-3 PAPERBACK 288P $15.95

Mysticism: Empowering the Spirit Within - "Fourteen Details for Immortal Medicine" is a chapter on meditation for women and men. Four other chapters are devoted to the study of 68 mystical diagrams, including the ones on Lao Tzu's tower. BMYST2 0-937064-46-7 PAPERBACK 200P $13.95

Internal Growth through Tao - In this volume, Hua-Ching Ni teaches about the more subtle, much deeper aspects of life. He also points out the confusion caused by some spiritual teachings and encourages students to cultivate internal growth. BINTE 0-937064-27-0 PAPERBACK 208P $13.95

Essence of Universal Spirituality - A review of world religions, revealing the harmony of their essence and helping readers enjoy the achievements of all religions without becoming confused by them. BESSE 0-937064-35-1 PAPERBACK 304P $19.95

Guide to Inner Light - Modern culture diverts our attention from our natural life being. Drawing inspiration from the experience of the ancient achieved ones, Hua-Ching Ni redirects modern people to their true source and to the meaning of life. BGUID 0-937064-30-0 PAPERBACK 192P $12.95

Stepping Stones for Spiritual Success - This volume contains practical and inspirational quotations from the traditional teachings of Tao. The societal values and personal virtues extolled here are relevant to any time or culture. BSTEP 0-937064-25-4 PAPERBACK 160P $12.95.

The Story of Two Kingdoms - The first part of this book is the metaphoric tale of the conflict between the Kingdoms of Light and Darkness. The second part details the steps to self-cleansing and self-confirmation. BSTOR 0-937064-24-6HARDCOVER 122P $14.50

The Gentle Path of Spiritual Progress - A companion volume to Messages of a Buffalo Rider. Hua-Ching Ni answers questions on contemporary psychology, sex, how to use the I Ching, and tells some fascinating spiritual legends! BGENT 0-937064-33-5 PAPERBACK 290P $12.95.

Footsteps of the Mystical Child - Profound examination of such issues as wisdom and spiritual evolution open new realms of understanding and personal growth. BFOOT 0-937064-11-4 PAPERBACK 166P $9.50

TIMELESS CLASSICS

The Complete Works of Lao Tzu - The *Tao Teh Ching* is one of the most widely translated and cherished works of literature. Its timeless wisdom provides a bridge to the subtle spiritual truth and aids harmonious and peaceful living. Plus the only authentic written translation of the *Hua Hu Ching*, a later work of Lao Tzu which was lost to the general public for a thousand years. BCOMP 0-937064-00-9 PAPERBACK 212P $13.95

The Book of Changes and the Unchanging Truth - Revised Edition - This version of the timeless classic *I Ching* is heralded as the standard for modern times. A unique presentation including profound illustrative commentary and details of the book's underlying natural science and philosophy from a world-renowned expert. BBOOK 0-937064-81-5 HARDCOVER 669P $35.00

Workbook for Spiritual Development - This is a practical, hands-on approach for those devoted to spiritual achievement. Diagrams show sitting postures, standing postures and even a sleeping cultivation. An entire section is devoted to ancient invocations. BWORK 0-937064-06-8 PAPERBACK 240P $14.95

The Esoteric Tao Teh Ching - This totally new edition offers instruction for studying the Tao Teh Ching and reveals the spiritual practices "hidden" in Lao Tzu's classic. These include in-depth techniques for advanced spiritual benefit. BESOT 0-937064-49-1 PAPERBACK 192P $13.95

The Way of Integral Life - The Universal Integral Way leads to a life of balance, health and harmony. This book includes practical suggestions for daily life, philosophical thought, esoteric insight and guidelines for those aspiring to help their lives and the world. BWAYS 0-937064-20-3 PAPERBACK 320P $14.00 • BWAYH 0-937064-21-1 HARDCOVER 320P $20.00.

Enlightenment: Mother of Spiritual Independence - The inspiring story and teachings of Hui Neng, the 6th Patriarch and father of Zen, highlight this volume. Intellectually unsophisticated, Hui Neng achieved himself to become a true spiritual revolutionary. BENLS 0-937064-19-X PAPERBACK 264P $12.50 • BENLH 0-937064-22-X HARDCOVER 264P $22.00.

Attaining Unlimited Life - Most scholars agree that Chuang Tzu produced some of the greatest literature in Chinese history. He also laid the foundation for the Universal Way. In this volume, Hua-Ching Ni draws upon his extensive training to rework the entire book of Chuang Tzu. BATTS 0-937064-18-1 PAPERBACK 467P $18.00; BATTH 0-937064-23-8 HARDCOVER $25.00

The Taoist Inner View of the Universe - This book offers a glimpse of the inner world and immortal realm known to achieved individuals and makes it understandable for students aspiring to a more complete life. BTAOI 0-937064-02-5 218P $14.95

Tao, the Subtle Universal Law - Thoughts and behavior evoke responses from the invisible net of universal energy. This book explains how self-discipline leads to harmony with the universal law. BTAOS 0-937064-01-7 PAPERBACK 208P $12.95

MUSIC AND MISCELLANEOUS

Colored Dust - Sung by Gaille. Poetry by Hua-Ching Ni. - The poetry of Hua-Ching Ni set to music creates a magical sense of transcendence through sound. 37 MINUTES ADUST CASSETTE $10.98, ADUST2 COMPACT DISC $15.95

Poster of Master Lu - Shown on cover of Workbook for Spiritual Development to be used in one's shrine. PMLTP 16" x 22" $10.95

POCKET BOOKLETS

Guide to Your Total Well-Being - Simple useful practices for self-development, aid for your spiritual growth and guidance for all aspects of life. Exercise, food, sex, emotional balancing, meditation. BWELL 0-937064-78-5 PAPERBACK 48P $4.00

Progress Along the Way: Life, Service and Realization - The guiding power of human life is the association between the developed mind and the achieved soul which contains love, rationality, conscience and everlasting value. BPROG 0-937-064-79-3 PAPERBACK 64P $4.00

The Light of All Stars Illuminates the Way - Through generations of searching, various achieved ones found the best application of the Way in their lives. This booklet contains their discovery. BSTAR 0-937064-80-7 48P $4.00

Less Stress, More Happiness - Helpful information for identifying and relieving stress in your life including useful techniques such as invocations, breathing and relaxation, meditation, exercise, nutrition and lifestyle balancing. BLESS 0-937064-55-06 48P $3.00

Integral Nutrition - Nutrition is an integral part of a healthy, natural life. Includes information on how to assess your basic body type, food preparation, energetic properties of food, nutrition and digestion. BNUTR 0-937064-84-X 32P $3.00

The Heavenly Way - Straighten Your Way (*Tai Shan Kan Yin Pien*) and The Silent Way of Blessing (*Yin Chia Wen*) are the main sources of inspiration for this booklet that sets the cornerstone for a mature, healthy life. BHEAV 0-937064-03-3 PAPERBACK 42P $2.50

HEALTH AND HEALING

Power of Natural Healing - This book is for anyone wanting to heal themselves or others. Methods include revitalization with acupuncture and herbs, *Tai Chi, Chi Kung (Chi Gong)*, sound, color, movement, visualization and meditation. BHEAL 0-937064-31-9 PAPERBACK 230P $14.95

Attune Your Body with *Dao-In* - The ancient Taoist predecessor to *Tai Chi Chuan*, these movements can be performed sitting and lying down to guide and refine your energy. Includes meditations and massage for a complete integral fitness program. To be used in conjunction with the video. BDAOI 0-937065-40-8 PAPERBACK WITH PHOTOGRAPHS 144P $14.95

101 Vegetarian Delights - by Lily Chuang and Cathy McNease - A lovely cookbook with recipes as tasty as they are healthy. Features multi-cultural recipes, appendices on Chinese herbs and edible flowers and a glossary of special foods. Over 40 illustrations. B101v 0-937064-13-0 PAPERBACK 176P $12.95

The Tao of Nutrition - by Maoshing Ni, Ph.D., with Cathy McNease, B.S., M.H. - Learn how to take control of your health with good eating. Over 100 common foods are discussed with their energetic properties and therapeutic functions listed. Food remedies for numerous common ailments are also presented. BNUTR 0-937064-66-1 PAPERBACK 214P $14.50

Chinese Vegetarian Delights - by Lily Chuang - An.extraordinary collection of recipes based on principles of traditional Chinese nutrition. Meat, sugar, dairy products and fried foods are excluded. BCHIV 0-937064-13-0 PAPERBACK 104P $7.50

Chinese Herbology Made Easy - by Maoshing Ni, Ph.D. - This text provides an overview of Oriental medical theory, in-depth descriptions of each herb category, over 300 black and white photographs, extensive tables of individual herbs for easy reference and an index of pharmaceutical names. BCHIH 0-937064-12-2 PAPERBACK 202P $14.50

Crane Style Chi Gong Book - By Daoshing Ni, Ph.D. - Standing meditative exercises practiced for healing. Combines breathing techniques, movement, and mental imagery to guide the smooth flow of energy. To be used with or without the videotape. BCRAN 0-937064-10-6 SPIRAL-BOUND 55P $10.95

VIDEOTAPES

Natural Living and the Universal Way (VHS) - *New!* - Interview of Hua-Ching Ni in the show "Asian-American Focus" hosted by Lily Chu. Dialogue on common issues of everyday life and practical wisdom. VINTE VHS VIDEO 30 MINUTES $15.95

Movement Arts for Emotional Health (VHS) -*New!* - Interview of Hua-Ching Ni in the show "Asian-American Focus" hosted by Lily Chu. Dialogue on emotional health and energy exercise that are fundamental to health and well-being. VMOVE VHS VIDEO 30 MINUTES $15.95

Attune Your Body with *Dao-In* (VHS) - by Master Hua-Ching Ni. - The ancient Taoist predecessor to *Tai Chi Chuan*. Performed sitting and lying down, these moves unblock, guide and refine energy. Includes meditations and massage for a complete integral fitness program. VDAOI VHS VIDEO 60 MINUTES $39.95

***T'ai Chi Ch'uan*: An Appreciation (VHS)** - by Hua-Ching Ni. - "Gentle Path," "Sky Journey" and "Infinite Expansion" are three esoteric styles handed down by highly achieved masters and are shown in an uninterrupted format. Not an instructional video. VAPPR VHS VIDEO 30 MINUTES $24.95

Self-Healing *Chi Gong* (VHS Video) - Strengthen your own self-healing powers. These effective mind-body exercises strengthen and balance each of your five major organ systems. Two hours of practical demonstrations and information lectures. VSHCG VHS VIDEO 120 MINUTES $39.95

Crane Style *Chi Gong* (VHS) - by Dr. Daoshing Ni, Ph.D. - These ancient exercises are practiced for healing purposes. They integrate movement, mental imagery and breathing techniques. To be used with the book. VCRAN VHS VIDEO 120 MINUTES $39.95

Taoist Eight Treasures (VHS) - By Maoshing Ni, Ph.D. - Unique to the Ni family, these 32 exercises open and refine the energy flow and strengthen one's vitality. Combines stretching, toning and energy conducting with deep breathing Book also available. VEIGH VHS VIDEO 105 MINUTES $39.95

***T'ai Chi Ch'uan* I & II (VHS)** - By Maoshing Ni, Ph.D. - This style, called the style of Harmony, is a distillation of the Yang, Chen and Wu styles. It integrates physical movement with internal energy and helps promote longevity and self-cultivation. VTAI1 VHS VIDEO PART 1 60 MINUTES $39.95 • VTAI2 VHS VIDEO PART 2 60 MINUTES $39.95

AUDIO CASSETTES

Invocations for Health, Longevity and Healing a Broken Heart - By Maoshing Ni, Ph.D. - "Thinking is louder than thunder." This cassette guides you through a series of invocations to channel and conduct your own healing energy and vital force. AINVO AUDIO 30 MINUTES $9.95

Stress Release with Chi Gong - By Maoshing Ni, Ph.D. - This audio cassette guides you through simple breathing techniques that enable you to release stress and tension that are a common cause of illness today. ACHIS AUDIO 30 MINUTES $9.95

Pain Management with Chi Gong - By Maoshing Ni, Ph.D. - Using visualization and deep-breathing techniques, this cassette offers methods for overcoming pain by invigorating your energy flow and unblocking obstructions that cause pain. ACHIP AUDIO 30 MINUTES $9.95

Tao Teh Ching Cassette Tapes - The classic work of Lao Tzu in this two-cassette set is a companion to the book translated by Hua-Ching Ni. Professionally recorded and read by Robert Rudelson. ATAOT 120 MINUTES $12.95

BOOKS IN SPANISH

Tao Teh Ching - En Español. BSPAN 0-937064-92-0 PAPERBACK 112 P $8.95

Now Visit SevenStar Communications
on the World Wide Web!
Our home page address is http://www.taostar.com

Order Form

SEVEN STAR
STAR
COMMUNICATIONS

name _____

street address _____

city _____ state _____ zip _____

country _____ best time to call _____

phone (day) _____ (evening) _____

Credit Card Information (VISA or MasterCard Only)

Credit Card No. _____

Exp. Date _____

Signature _____

Quantity	Price	Title	5 Letter Code	Total

Sub total _____

Sales tax (CA residents only, 8.25%) _____

Shipping (see left) _____

Total Amount Enclosed _____

Mail this form with payment
(US funds only) to:

SevenStar Communications
1314 Second Street
Santa Monica, CA 90401 USA

Credit Card Orders:
call **1-800-578-9526**
or fax **310-917-2267**

E-Mail Orders:
taostar@ix.netcom.com

Other Inquiries
1-310-576-1901

Shipping Charges

Number of items	Domestic		International			
	UPS Ground	4th Class Book Rate US Mail	Surface US Mail	Air [2] Printed Matter US Mail	Air Parcel Rate US Mail	UPS Int'l Air
First item [1]	4.50	2.00	2.50	7.50	12.00	46.00
Each Additional item	0.50	0.50	1.00	5.00[3]	6.00	6.00

NOTES
1 BOOK OF CHANGES (I CHING) because of weight, counts as 3 items, all other books count as one item each.
2 US Mail Air Printed Matter Table to be used for European destination only. All others use Parcel rate.
3 Limit of 4 items only for this service.

DELIVERY TIMES
UPS Ground: 7-10 days, Insured
4th Class Book Rate USmail: 5-8 week, Uninsured
Surface US mail (Overseas): 6-9 weeks, Uninsured
Air Printed Matter USmail (Overseas): 2-4 weeks, Uninsured
Air Parcel Rate USmail: 2-4 weeks, Insured
UPS International Air: 4 days, Insured

Spiritual Study and Teaching
Through the College of Tao

The College of Tao (COT) and the Union of Tao and Man were formally established in California in the 1970's, yet this tradition is a very broad spiritual culture containing centuries of human spiritual growth. Its central goal is to offer healthy spiritual education to all people to help individuals develop themselves for a spiritually developed world. This time-tested "school without walls" values the spiritual development of each individual self and passes down its guidance and experience.

COT does not use an institution with a building. Human society is its classroom. Your own life and service are the class you attend; thus students learn from their lives and from studying the guidance of the Universal Way.

Any interested individual is welcome to join and learn for oneself. The Self-Study Program that is based on Master Ni's books and videotapes gives people who wish to study on their own, or are too far from a teacher, an opportunity to study the Universal Way. The outline for the Self-Study Program is given in the book *The Golden Message*. If you choose, a Correspondence Course is also available.

A Mentor is any individual who is spiritually self-responsible and who is a model of a healthy and complete life. A Mentor may serve as a teacher for general society and people with a preliminary interest in spiritual development. To be certified to teach, a Mentor must first register with the Universal Society of the Integral Way (USIW) and follow the Mentor Service Handbook, which was written by Mentors. It is recommended that all prospective Mentors use the Correspondence Course or self-study program to educate themselves, but they may also learn directly from other Mentors. COT offers special seminars taught only to Mentors.

If you are interested in the Integral Way of Life Correspondence Course, please write: College of Tao, PO Box 1222, El Prado, NM 87529 USA.

- -

If you would like more information about the USIW and classes in your area, please send the following form to: USIW, PO Box 28993, Atlanta, GA 30358-0993 USA

☐ I wish to be put on the mailing list of the USIW to be notified of educational activities.

☐ I wish to receive a list of Registered Mentors teaching in my area or country.

☐ I am interested in joining/forming a study group in my area.

☐ I am interested in becoming a member or Mentor of the USIW.

Name:_____

Address:_____

City:_____State:_____Zip:_____

Country:_____

Phone, Fax and/or E-mail_____

Herbs Used by Ancient Masters

The pursuit of everlasting youth or immortality throughout human history is an innate human desire. Long ago, Chinese esoteric Taoists went to the high mountains to contemplate nature, strengthen their bodies, empower their minds and develop their spirits. From their studies and cultivation, they gave China alchemy and chemistry, herbology and acupuncture, the I Ching, astrology, martial arts and T'ai Chi Ch'uan, Chi Gong and many other useful kinds of knowledge.

Most important, they handed down in secrecy methods for attaining longevity and spiritual immortality. There were different levels of approach; one was to use a collection of food herb formulas available only to highly achieved Taoist masters. They used these food herbs to increase energy and heighten vitality. This treasured collection of herbal formulas remained within the Ni family for centuries.

Now, through Traditions of Tao, the Ni family makes these foods available for you to use to assist the foundation of your own positive development. It is only with a strong foundation that expected results are produced from diligent cultivation.

As a further benefit, in concert with the Taoist principle of self-sufficiency, Traditions of Tao offers the food herbs along with SevenStar Communication's publications in a distribution opportunity for anyone serious about financial independence.

Send to: *Traditions of Tao*
              1314 Second Street #200
              Santa Monica, CA 90401

Please send me a Traditions of Tao brochure.

Name _____

Address _____

City _____ *State* _____ *Zip* _____

Phone (day) _____ *(evening)* _____

Yo San University of Traditional Chinese Medicine

"Not just a medical career, but a life-time commitment to raising one's spiritual standard."

Thank you for your support and interest in our publications and services. It is by your patronage that we continue to offer you the practical knowledge and wisdom from this venerable Taoist tradition.

Because of your sustained interest in natural health, in January 1989 we formed Yo San University of Traditional Chinese Medicine, a non-profit educational institution under the direction of founder Master Ni, Hua-Ching. Yo San University is the continuation of 38 generations of Ni family practitioners who handed down their knowledge and wisdom. Its purpose is to train and graduate practitioners of the highest caliber in Traditional Chinese Medicine, which includes acupuncture, herbology and spiritual development.

We view Traditional Chinese Medicine as the application of spiritual development. Its foundation is the spiritual capability to know life, diagnose a person's problem and cure it. We teach students how to care for themselves and others, emphasizing the integration of traditional knowledge and modern science. Yo San University offers a complete accredited Master's degree program approved by the California State Department of Education that provides an excellent education in Traditional Chinese Medicine and meets all requirements for state licensure. Federal financial aid and scholarships are available, and we accept students from all countries.

We invite you to inquire into our university for a creative and rewarding career as a holistic physician. Classes are also open to persons interested in self-enrichment. For more information, please fill out the form below and send it to:

> Yo San University of Traditional Chinese Medicine
> 1314 Second Street
> Santa Monica, CA 90401 U.S.A.

❑   Please send me information on the Masters degree program in Traditional Chinese Medicine.

❑   Please send me information on the massage certificate program.

❑   Please send me information on health workshops and seminars.

❑   Please send me information on continuing education for acupuncturists and health professionals.

Name _____

Address _____

City _____ *State* _____ *Zip* _____

Phone (day) _____ *(evening)* _____

Glossary

Note: For details and descriptions of acupuncture channels and points, please see Chapter 7.

<u>Acupuncture:</u> A therapeutic technique of Traditional Chinese Medicine whereby points on the body's surface are stimulated to effect the physiological functioning of the whole body or specific parts. Points are stimulated by insertion of very fine needles, applying heat through moxabustion, or pressure.

<u>*Ba Gong Dao-In, Pa Gong Dao-In* or *Pa Kun Dao-In*</u>: Another name for the Eight Treasures which is translated into English as "eight treasures of the immortal tradition," "energy conducting exercises of the eight old ones," or "channelling exercise of your body energy from the eight achieved ones."

<u>Beak position:</u> A hand position formed by putting the tips of the fingers and tip of the thumb together in a point.

<u>Channels:</u> Distinct pathways of energy flow in the human body.

<u>*Chi (Qi* or *Ki)*</u>: *Chi* is the vitality or life energy of the universe and resides within each living being. Along with *jing* and *shen*, it is one of the "three treasures" of natural life cultivation. *Chi* is a fundamental substance which exists at different levels of refinement, enabling all function, activity and warmth. In humans, it provides the power for our movements of body and mind, immune system and all organ functions. The sources of *chi* are our inherited constitution (pre-heaven) and our environment through diet and exercise (post-heaven). In *chi gong* practice, we train to optimally gather, activate and store this precious resource.

<u>*Chi gong, (chi kung* or *qi gong)*</u>: Translated literally as "energy work," "energy exercise," or "breathing exercise." A set of breathing, movement and/or visualization exercises for strengthening and balancing the *chi* or vital force, relaxing the mind, maintaining health and curing disease. Can be static (no movement) or dynamic (with movement). It is usually a single exercise or a small group of exercises practiced separately or together.

<u>Confucius:</u> Also expressed in Chinese as Kung Fu Tze or Kung Fu Tse. Achieved master who continued the ancient humanistic teaching. (551-479 B.C.E.)

185

Control Points: see Points.

Dao-In: A series of movements traditionally used for conducting physical energy. Solves problems of stagnant energy, increases health, lengthens one's years, and provides support for cultivation and higher achievements of spiritual immortality. May be used to refer to a specific set of movements which are done indoors sitting and lying on a mat.

Eight Treasures™: A form of *Dao-In*, a type of internal exercise or *chi kung* (*chi gong*) patterned after natural movements.

Fu Shi (or Fu Hsi): Ancient one who developed a "line system" to express the principle of appropriateness, which is the basis of the present *I Ching*. Active around 2852-2739 B.C.E..

Huai Nan Zi (or Huey Nang Tzu): Another name for Prince Liu Ahn. Also *Huai Nan Zi* is used to refer to a book written by Prince Liu Ahn; its first part is called *Huai Nan Zi*, and the second part was entitled *Ten Thousand Year's Treasure*. See Liu Ahn.

I Ching (or *I Jing*): A method of divination which uses 64 hexagrams. Information about the hexagrams, their interpretation, and commentary about the changes and unchanging truth of nature, human society, and individual life, was recorded in an ancient book by the same name, which is translated into English as *The Book of Changes*. As a system of divination, the *I Ching* can help you respond appropriately to the changes in your own life.

Jing (or *ching*): Watery essence of the body, derived from the parents' sexual union (pre-Heaven essence), refined and extracted from food and fluids by the Stomach and Spleen (post-Heaven essence), and derived from the interaction of the pre-Heaven and post-Heaven essence (Kidney essence). Important for growth, reproduction and development, forms the basis of Kidney *chi*, produces marrow, and is the basis of constitutional strength. Related to and stored in the kidneys.

Kou Hong: Achieved master. Also known in Chinese as Bao Boh Tzu or Pao Poh Tzu. For information see *Life and Teaching of Two Immortals: Volume I*.

Lao Tzu: Also expressed in Chinese as Lao Zi, Lao Tze or Lao Tse.

Achieved master who continued the teaching of natural truth and the importance of sincerity in universal life. Author of the *Tao Teh Ching* and *Hua Hu Ching*. (Active around 571 B.C.E.)

Liu Ahn: Prince and grandson of the first emperor of Han (active around 178-122 B.C.E.). Also known as Huai Nan Zi.

Lower *Tan Tien:* See *Tan Tien.*

Meditation: Usually a time dedicated to being undisturbed by the world in order to quiet the mind and go deeply within oneself. This may be done sitting, standing, lying, or moving.

Middle *Tan Tien:* See *Tan Tien.*

Niao: Chinese emperor (2357-2258 B.C.E.)

Organ System: In Traditional Chinese Medicine, the interrelationship of internal organs and their corresponding energies. Organs in an energy system are usually considered paired, such as the western stomach and spleen comprise the Chinese Stomach System.

Pao Poh Tzu: See Kou Hong.

Peng Zhu: Long-lived, achieved master, reputed to have lived for 800 years.

Points: Specific locations on channels that can effectively and predictably manipulate the flow of energy in the human body.

San Jiao: Translated as Triple Warmer, Three Warmers or Triple Heater, which are the three cavities in the chest and abdomen which keep the body warm.

Shen or *Sen*: The spiritual essence of the mind. Derived from the interaction of *jing* and *chi*, which provide a stronger or weaker basis for *shen*. Related to, and often referred to being housed in the heart.

Shien Jia Ba Duan Jin: Another name for the Eight Treasures. Translated as Eight Groups of Exercises From the Immortal School.

Shien: An immortal, a spiritually achieved individual.

Shun: Chinese emperor (2257-2208 B.C.E.)

T'ai Chi Movement (sometimes called *T'ai Chi Chuan* or *Tai Ji Quan*): Ancient Chinese exercise for harmonizing mind, body and spirit, whose connected movements somewhat resemble a graceful dance. Consists of many different *chi gong* movements put together sequentially and arranged with the principles given by the *Tao Teh Ching* and *I Ching*. Practiced for spiritual and health purposes, not for martial intent.

T'ai Chi Principle: The principle of harmonization of alternating opposites, also called the *Yin/Yang* Principle, the Universal Law, or the Law of *T'ai Chi*.

T'ai Chi Symbol: A symbol depicting the balance of *yin* and *yang*.

Tan Tien (or Dan Tien): *Tan tien* is a term which is used generically to refer to several energy centers of the body where energy is stored, within the context of personal energy cultivation: the Upper *Tan Tien* (Heavenly Eye Point or *Tien Mu,* not associated with a channel), the Middle *Tan Tien* (Heart Center or the area around *Ren* 17), and the Lower *Tan Tien* area. It is also used specifically to refer to the Lower Tan Tien and is translated as Field of Elixir. Located about four finger widths below the navel. This is more an area than a specific point on the body, being generally in the area of the *Ren* 4, *Ren* 5 and *Ren* 6 points. For a diagram showing the locations of the *tan tien,* see Figure 48, page 99.

Tao (or Dao): The Integral Way. The profound truth of life.

Tao Teh Ching (or Dao Deh Jing): An influential book which was written by Lao Tzu as an attempt to describe Tao, the subtle truth of life. Considered a Taoist classic, it is among the most widely translated and distributed books in the world.

Three Warmers, Triple Warmer, or Triple Heater: see *San Jiao*.

Traditional Chinese Medicine: An integral system of healing designed to balance the interrelationship of the human body, mind, and spirit. This is accomplished through the skilled use of acupuncture, herbs, *chi kung,* massage, gentle movement, and meditation.

Upper *Tan Tien:* See *Tan Tien.*

Virtue: A balanced way of life achieved by avoiding extremes and living in accordance with the Subtle Universal Law. A human characteristic or personality trait of high morality.

Wu Wei: The principle of "doing nothing extra," "doing just enough," "non-doing," "harmonious action," or "effortless activity."

Wu: Chinese emperor (108-86 B.C.E.) during the Han dynasty, and nephew of Prince Liu Ahn

Xian Tien Zhi Chi: translated as pre-natal *chi,* ancestral *chi,* or pre-Heaven *chi.* See *chi.*

Yang: Relating to the male, outward, active, positive, fiery, energetic side of life or nature of a person. Derived from an ancient Chinese character representing "the sunny side of a hill."

Yin: Relating to the female, inward, passive, negative, watery, cool, substantial side of life or nature of a person. Derived from an ancient Chinese character representing "the shady side of a hill."

Yin and *Yang:* Terms which describe opposites, compliments, the two ends of either pole, or duality.

Yu: Chinese emperor (2207-2197 B.C.E.) Also referred to as "The Great Yu" for his selfless service in controlling the recurring, devastating floods in ancient China.

Index